PRAISE FOR
my HEALTHY d

"My's recipes are mouthwatering, beautiful, and so nourishing for your body! She knows what it takes to make cooking easy and healthy for anyone with a busy schedule. So, no excuses!"

—Cassey Ho, creator of POP Pilates

"This book makes it seem so simple—eating healthy for the entire family. After reading, anyone can make delicious and nutritious meals that their family will love!"

—Kelly Plowe, MS, RD, CSSD, Livestrong.com dietitian and nutrition expert

My Healthy Dish is my go-to resource for simple meal recipes that my entire family loves. I love how flavorful and quick the recipes are. Not only are the ingredients easy to find at my local grocery store, but this book makes healthy eating a part of my everyday lifestyle."

—Jadah Sellner, author and cofounder of Simple Green Smoothies

"*My Healthy Dish* brings cookable recipes for the busy but health-conscious mom. The ingredients are often what you already have in your pantry, the directions are simple, and the entire family enjoys it. Finally, an easy cookbook for an everyday working family."

—Maria Kang, founder of No Excuse Mom and author of *The No More Excuses Diet*

"[Nguyen is] refreshingly forthright about her lifestyle philosophy and her own encounters with food. Readers will be drawn into her life almost instantly as she begins the book with a preface chronicling a day in her life. The book's real guts are in the recipe pages. . . . Nguyen is a great spokeswoman for everything in moderation."

—*Booklist*

my **HEALTHY** dish

Simple, Delicious & Nutritious Recipes for the Whole Family

MY NGUYEN

Creator of MyHealthyDish.com

Skyhorse Publishing

Skyhorse Publishing books may be purchased in bulk at special discounts for sales promotion, corporate gifts, fund-raising, or educational purposes. Special editions can also be created to specifications. For details, contact the Special Sales Department, Skyhorse Publishing, 307 West 36th Street, 11th Floor, New York, NY 10018 or info@skyhorsepublishing.com.

Skyhorse® and Skyhorse Publishing® are registered trademarks of Skyhorse Publishing, Inc.®, a Delaware corporation.

Visit our website at www.skyhorsepublishing.com.

10 9 8 7 6 5 4 3 2 1

Library of Congress Cataloging-in-Publication Data is available on file.

Cover design by David Ter-Avenesyan
Cover photographs by Tuan Nguyen of TN Photography and author

Paperback ISBN: 978-1-5107-7421-6
Hardcover ISBN: 978-1-5107-0343-8
Ebook ISBN: 978-1-5107-0344-5

Printed in China

*This book is dedicated to my very patient husband, Harlen,
and my heart and soul, Shayna and Kiera. I wouldn't be the woman
I am today without their love and support.*

CONTENTS

My Story   01

A Day in the Life   13

So, What's Healthy?   19

What's in My Kitchen?   27

Recipes

Breakfast   **29**

Soups, Sides & Sauces   **49**

Lunch & Dinner   **85**

Meal Prepping with Slow Cooker Dinners   **129**

Smoothies, Shakes & Desserts   **143**

Acknowledgments   **172**

Index   **175**

Conversion Charts   **183**

MY STORY

"Excuse me, are you *My Healthy Dish*?" That's a common question I get asked these days when I leave the house. I know it's odd to say, but it's one of my biggest accomplishments—not to be referred to as My Nguyen. Don't get me wrong; I love my given name and I am very proud to be a Nguyen. The accomplishment I'm referring to is being recognized as *My Healthy Dish*, a screen name I gave myself on Instagram. A social media account that I single-handedly grew to over one million followers in less than two years launched a career for me I didn't know was possible. I did it from sharing my passion for food, cooking, health, and my life. How it all came to be was a simple act of fate.

I was born in Vietnam in 1980. From there, I immigrated to the United States when I was three, went to school, graduated college with a Communications degree, worked a desk job in mortgage financing, married my college boyfriend, and bought our first house. As a first-generation immigrant, I believed in the American Dream, something instilled in me from my parents. I was unhappy at my job, but I accepted this as the norm because,

honestly, who likes to work? Work was not meant to be fun, right? I knew I wasn't the only one looking forward to 5 p.m. on Fridays and dreading 8 a.m. on Mondays. It wasn't until I lost my job that I realized there was something seriously wrong simply accepting this line of thinking.

Being set free from my job was like being freed from a prison of my own making. At first, I woke up every morning feeling lost. I had relearn myself and figure out what made me tick. To be honest, it was quite depressing because I had forgotten what made me happy. After years at a job I hated, I had nothing that brought me joy. I had a big, five-bedroom house for only the two of us, a collection of Louis Vuitton purses I wore to be envied, a 1.5-carat diamond ring that cost my husband six months of pay, a Mercedes in my driveway, and a closet full of designer clothes and shoes. That's what I thought made me happy, but I was delusional. I hated my job, and I had bought all those things to justify working there. I always thought that work was something we had to do and our passions were our hobbies. Turns out, losing my job gave me the freedom to pursue my passion. My motivator this time was not money, but happiness.

In 2007, my husband, Harlen, and I bought our first house, and in 2008, we lost our jobs and the house, got pregnant with twins, and moved in with my parents! As bad as that sounds, looking back, it was the best thing that ever happened to us. You see, after years of trying to get pregnant and suffering a heartbreaking miscarriage, we were blessed with twins. I had been working sixty hours a week and had been under an extreme amount of stress because of it. Being unemployed and having nothing better to do than make babies, we got pregnant in no time at all. My husband eventually went back to work before Shayna and Kiera were born, and we decided it was best for me to stay at home with the girls. I traded in the Mercedes for a used Chevy Malibu, sold what we could, and stored the rest until we were back on our feet.

Still, the needs of growing babies took a financial toll on us. By the time the twins were three, getting a job weighed heavily on my mind. I wanted to help provide for my family, but I couldn't stand the idea of leaving them. Buying us some time, I held a garage sale to get rid of all the girls' baby stuff. We made so much money, we decided to join the twenty-first century and trade in our Razor flip phones for iPhones. As I'm technically challenged, it was really hard for my husband to convince

me to get them, but I'm sure glad I did. The iPhone turned out to be the answer to my prayers.

Who ever thought that phones were for more than just for phone calls? Did you know you have more technology in the palm of your hand than NASA had for their first shuttle launch? With the world at my fingertips, I did what any normal human being would do: I downloaded Angry Birds and Instagram. I was instantly hooked, not on the mean birds, but on IG. Being Asian, it's intrinsically in my DNA to take pictures of everything. My family and friends got inundated all day with photos of the twins waking up, eating breakfast, crying, smiling, walking, napping, sitting, standing and, once in a while, they also saw the food I cooked. Then the oddest thing happened: I was receiving more interest in my food than the pictures of the twins, and my girls are pretty darn cute. I was extremely flattered that so many people took to my food. Cooking had become a creative outlet for me.

My following grew and soon strangers started asking for my recipes. When my following grew to five hundred, I felt like the popular new kid on IG. (In your face, old high-school me!) This small success helped me decide to take a leap of faith and start food blogging. I knew there had to be a way to make a little money from it. I borrowed $1,500 from my mom for a MacBook and sacrificed my precious sleep

to build *My Healthy Dish*. I didn't have a sure plan or any idea what bloggers really did, so I focused most of my time on Instagram. I changed my username to @Myhealthydish_ and started posting recipes and health advice every day. In three months, my loyal five hundred followers grew to thirty thousand. After that milestone, I launched my blog MyHealthyDish.com. I then went on to celebrate one million followers within two years. I thought I was so cool at five hundred followers, but at one million, I felt like Britney Spears before she shaved her head. I know what you're thinking: what makes me so awesome that people wanted to follow? As much as I would love to believe they're following for pics of me, I know it's my recipes people love and not my #selfies.

I once watched an episode of *Shark Tank* where one of the sharks, Lori Grenier, said that the most successful entrepreneurs are the ones who solve problems. I mean, look at the Snuggie. Who would've thought a blanket with sleeves would turn out to be a multi-million dollar idea? Even I felt compelled to steal one at my best friend's annual White Elephant party. It's pure genius—now I can read in bed and flip through the channels without my arms getting cold. Although it's not the life-changing Snuggie, my page was solving one the biggest problems people struggle with today. Let's face facts: Americans are really unhealthy and fat. Yes, I said the word *fat*. I know that word is sensitive to a lot of people, but it's the truth.

The Snuggie solved a problem in such a simple way, and my page is doing the same. People want to be healthy, but they are doing it all wrong. They are falling into traps of fad diets and consuming more processed foods now than ever before. How did we get to this point where we're cooking less and reheating more? My guess is that the high cost of living in the United States requires a two-income household now. With both parents working, who's at home cooking? Isn't it easier to pick up something fast on the way home or throw in a frozen pizza than to cook a dinner after a long day at the office?

Really think about it next time you're at the grocery store. Make an observation of which one-ingredient foods are sitting in your cart. Pick up a package and try to pronounce all the ingredients listed. Would someone who lived one hundred years ago recognize what was in your cart? Are you buying these foods out of convenience or health? The sad part is we are losing a bit of our family history with each generation. No longer are we passing down grandma's homemade pot roast recipe; all we're passing down to our children are stacks of take-out menus and re-heating instructions. (Not to mention obesity, diabetes, high cholesterol, and a shorter life expectancy.) People follow me because they want to change that for themselves and for their families.

What *My Healthy Dish* offered was a realistic approach to a healthy lifestyle. I didn't preach diets, detox, cleanses, or nominate anyone for the Hunger Games. Every day, I showed people what healthy food really is. Through my recipes, I offered easy-to-prepare meals for the family. I even showed shortcuts and cost-effective meals to save time and money. Most importantly, I proved that eating healthy is delicious. I always say to my followers, "If eating healthy is hard, then you're doing it wrong." That's it! I know that sounds simple, but so was putting sleeves on a blanket.

If Instagram is a window, then my followers are peeping toms. I inspire people to be healthy just by showing my real life and real food. Even if that means dirty dishes in the sink, my cheat meals to In-N-Out Burger, or my grocery haul from Costco. I'm not a trained chef, nutritionist, or health coach. My expertise in those categories comes from my life experience. Truth is, we all have an idea of what's healthy. You don't have to go to Rocket Science School to know vegetables are good, potato chips are bad. That's not the problem anymore. Food has changed so much from its original form that it's hard to decipher what's healthy.

This is what I learned from dealing with my own weight and health issues.

In my freshmen year of college, I did not put on the requisite fifteen pounds—I put on more than thirty. What can I say? I've always been an overachiever. It was a lot to add on in such a short amount of time and, being Snookie height, it really showed. As hard as I tried to lose weight and keep it off, I just couldn't. I tried low carb, low calorie, South Beach, meal replacement shakes, cleanses, and a few more ideas I'm not too proud of. I think the worst one was replacing a meal a day with a chocolate Slimfast shake. I even did the Subway diet. Every day after class, I would pick up a six-inch cold cut trio on wheat, with baked Ruffles potato chips and a diet coke. Had I known then what I know now about processed meats and diet sodas, I never would've allowed all those chemicals in my body.

I think the worst diet I tried was a fat-free diet. Don't be fooled into fat-free or low-fat foods. It sounded so logical at the time: cutting fat out of my diet would result in cutting fat out of my body. With that mission in mind, I went to the grocery store and bought anything that said fat-free or low-fat. Looking back on my grocery list now makes me sad. It consisted of everything fat-free or low-fat—bread, cheese, turkey, mayonnaise, crackers, etc. I didn't have much real food in my shopping cart. It was all processed foods. I had no clue what I was doing and, needless to say, it all tasted like crap. I stuck to it for a few weeks and it didn't work. Not only did I not lose weight, but I think I gained a few pounds. What I didn't know then was that, to compensate for less fat, most manufacturers add more sugar. I was consuming more sugar which, ironically, turns into fat! Yes, that bag of fat-free gummy bears is too good to be true.

Once again, being clueless in nutrition at the time, I did not know that sugar came in many forms. I did not know that bread and pasta are also forms of sugar, or to be more correct, once consumed, turn into glucose, which is a simple sugar our bodies use for energy. When you eat a carbohydrate, your blood sugar levels increase because your body metabolizes it into glucose. Glucose is our main source of energy. Insulin is secreted from the pancreas to carry the glucose from the bloodstream into cells to use for energy. The higher a food is in the glycemic index, the faster it raises your blood sugar levels. Foods composed of refined sugars, such as candy, have little to no nutritional value and release glucose more quickly. If there's too much glucose, your blood sugar levels increase dramatically and your pancreas goes into overdrive, releasing more insulin to draw the sugar out of your blood stream and storing the excess as fat. This also results in blood sugar levels dropping dramatically, causing more hunger. Just like your body needs fat, it also needs sugar. Glucose is our main source of energy, but excess sugar or unused energy is stored as fat.

With each failed attempt, the number on the scale grew bigger and my clothes felt like they were getting smaller. I knew I had to do something because I could barely afford my schoolbooks, let alone new clothes. Living in my boyfriend's (now husband) sweatpants was not an option; it was only cute for a quick minute. It finally became apparent to me what I was doing wrong: I wasn't eating real food anymore. You see, I was lucky I grew up poor! Yeah, I said that right. I didn't feel lucky at the time, though.

I was born in Vietnam in 1980 and was fortunate enough to leave as a refugee when I was two with my family and my aunt's family. We lived in the Philippines at a refugee camp for a year before finally coming to the United States. My parents chose to come to New York City because my aunt and uncle had settled there a few months prior. It was a huge shock, coming from Vietnam and arriving in the middle of winter in New York City. After ten days of being human popsicles, we hightailed it to sunny California. My family had friends in Los Angeles to stay with, and they helped us get acclimated with the new language and culture. Once we were settled, we were so financially challenged that my parents couldn't afford to take us out to eat. I know the irony of this, but going to McDonald's felt like Christmas, and I still feel giddy when I indulge in a Big Mac.

The one time my parents took us out to an American restaurant was a complete disaster. Even though I was very young, the memory of it is still imprinted in my mind. My parents wanted to treat us to a nice dinner, so they took us to Denny's. During that time, they spoke little English and my siblings and I were too young to translate. The only thing the server understood from my parents from their finger pointing was that we wanted chicken. When our dinner came, it was a single plate of chicken. One meal for the six of us. My parents were so embarrassed from the ordering experience that we didn't go back to a restaurant that wasn't Vietnamese for years. At the time, my parents worked tirelessly day and night sewing garments to make money. It took a lot of time to save money to take us out to dinner, and it is heartbreaking to remember how humiliated they were.

Eventually my mom got her manicurist license and went to work, so my dad stayed home and cooked the majority of our meals. It wasn't salads and quinoa every day, but it was still real food. What I was eating in college was anything but that. I went from eating at home for almost every meal to fast food or packaged food every day. Those late-night Jack in the Box runs happened frequently during college. It was perfect—I studied late, didn't know how to cook, and could live off any fast-food dollar menu. It was a vicious cycle of junk food. I was tired more and more often because of all the unhealthy food I was putting in my body. I turned to sweets when I felt low on energy. It felt like I was addicted to sugar, and Milky Ways were my drug of choice. It was an addiction that was extremely hard to shake. The more I ate, the more I craved. So there I was my freshmen year of college, overweight, feeling sluggish, and unhappy with my body. I wanted to change, but didn't put in much effort. But then there was that one defining moment that finally pushed me down the right path. . . .

I was still very stubborn and cheap back then. I was refusing to waste money on a new pair of jeans, especially if it was going to have a size ten on the label. Instead, I went shopping for new boots and that's when it happened:

I had been wearing a pair of jeans that I literally had to jump and shimmy into, barely being able to zip and button close. I remember picking out a pair of knee-high black boots with a side zipper. I managed to kick off my running shoes, but to my embarrassment, I was unable to bend over to put on my boots. My jeans were so tight, it physically hurt to bend over. What was even more horrifying was having Harlen, my then-boyfriend, assist me with the boots while shoppers were watching. One of the girls passing by said it was so sweet he was kneeling down and assisting

me, but internally I felt so ashamed that I couldn't do it myself. I made the decision that day to start focusing on bettering myself. Instead of the boots, I bought the size-ten jeans and never looked back.

I made three life changes: I started cooking more, dining out less, and ate fewer packaged foods. The first step I took was learning how to cook. This was more than fifteen years ago, so I didn't have everything at my fingertips. Smartphones and Pinterest did not exist back then so I had to get my information the old-fashioned way: through dial-up Internet and The Food Network. I became obsessed with Rachael Ray and her show, *30 Minute Meals*. It is no coincidence that most of my recipes take about thirty minutes to make. I watched her daily just to get down the basics of cooking.

Second, I started premaking meals so I could save money and time. When I cooked, I usually made enough for a few meals. I went old school and started packing lunch to eat between classes. I still went on those late-night runs to Jack in the Box, but it was more as a treat than a necessity. Packing a sandwich and fruit turned out to be the same price, if not cheaper, than fast food.

Third and, the most important thing to me, was making sure that when I was cooking, I was using whole foods: meaning using one-ingredient foods as much as possible like chicken, broccoli, asparagus, and garlic. This is not to say that I didn't open a can of tomatoes to make pasta sauce, but when I used packaged foods I tried to read labels to make sure the ingredients were all natural. What I started noticing was that I was shopping more and more at the perimeter of the grocery store and less in the center isles. It makes perfect sense now: all the really perishable foods, like fruits and vegetables, were located around the perimeter of the store, and all the processed, preserved foods, like packaged foods, were in the center.

I should mention that I didn't live by these three changes consistently. These were goals to attain, but I didn't stress if I ended up having a pizza night with friends. What I learned from all the fad diets was that living with extreme restrictions only lasts as long as your will power. You have to find something that works long term. I came to the conclusion that being healthy is a lifestyle not a diet. With just those changes, I started feeling better and losing weight. I felt accomplished and was surprised to finally see results when all I was doing was eating real food.

Ann Wigmore once said: "The food you eat can be either the safest and most powerful form of medicine or the slowest form of poison." It's a quote that really resonated with me and will pop up in my mind occasionally when I'm eating. You see, I didn't realize I was categorizing foods based on why I was eating. I had two categories: nourishment or pleasure. This was the wrong way to look at food. By doing this, I was telling myself the food that brought me nourishment did not bring me pleasure. I believe a lot of people see food the same way. It wasn't until I started cooking for myself that I realized healthy food can be nourishing, but also a pleasure to eat. By combining them, I solved my weight and health problems.

I started this journey because I wanted to feel better and I wanted to put my health first. I started seeing results, but most importantly, I was feeling them. I remember always needing long naps and waking up feeling sluggish instead of reenergized. In the winter, my cheeks would be rosy red, dry, patchy, and extremely itchy. After I changed my diet, I got sick a lot less, had more energy, less acne, and no eczema breakouts. I can honestly say my skin looks healthier now in my thirties than it did in college.

The more I experimented in the kitchen and researched food, the more delicious and healthy my recipes became. I pride myself now about not compromising taste for the sake of eating something nutritious. (I still can't stand the taste of celery no matter how much peanut butter I dip it in.) When I became a mom, I kept that same philosophy. I was never going to force my family to eat broccoli if they didn't like it or not allow my kids to have pizza because it was unhealthy. It was about finding the right balance. To me, being healthy is a lifestyle that is

attainable and realistic. Pizza, of course, is not nutritious, but I believe allowing it is healthy. It's my way of fostering a healthy relationship between my kids and food.

I believe in fate, that if things are meant to happen, they will happen. If I didn't grow up poor, I wouldn't have seen the value of cooking at home. If I didn't put on all that weight in college, I wouldn't have learned how to cook for myself. If I didn't lose my house and job, I don't think Shayna and Kiera would be in my life. If it weren't for selling their old baby clothes at a garage sale, I never would have bought that iPhone and downloaded Instagram that fateful day. If I hadn't created *My Healthy Dish* on Instagram, I never would have found a job that I love and that I wake up excited about every morning.

This job gave new life to not only me, but my husband, also. He was so inspired about me pursuing a career I was passionate about, he quit his job and started his own video production company. We were able to move out of my parents' house into a neighborhood with amazing schools for the girls. My husband and I are now a team, developing cooking videos for *My Healthy Dish*. Sure, we bicker and get on each other's nerves because we are together 24/7, but deep down, I think we both enjoy the banter and the back and forth. It's pretty awesome to boss your husband around sometimes. Even though we work our butts off and our kitchen is always a disaster, it doesn't feel like work to us. Well, except when it's time to wash dishes.

A DAY IN THE LIFE

The most flattering compliments I get are from other parents. They say I'm Supermom because I balance career, family, and health. The feedback I get is that most parents sacrifice their health because career and family are the necessities. They see me working, exercising, volunteering at the girls' school, cheering them on at swim class, grocery shopping, cooking, and fitting in date nights, and they can either relate or they wonder how I can do it all. I think it's so important to really show the truth: this is not easy. Sometimes in the morning, I skip the gym and go back to bed because the night before my kids woke me up by repeatedly sneaking into my bed. I sometimes forget to brush my teeth in the midst of getting the girls to school on time. I'm late to everything and even missed my friend's wedding day because I just forgot it was happening. And, as healthy as I want my family to be, I will pack chips on a road trip to Disneyland because it's okay to splurge sometimes. I'm like every other parent out there and I think they appreciate the honesty instead of me portraying a perfect cookie-cutter life. Here's an example of one of my crazier days, back when we lived in 978 square feet.

7:30 a.m.
My phone alarm wakes me up to Taylor Swift's perky voice singing "Shake it Off." I have one daughter snuggled against my back and my other daughter draped across my feet. Somehow the whole right side of the bed is empty. I can hear my husband snoring from the twins' room, having stumbled there sometime during our nightly game of musical beds. I reluctantly crawl out of my California king bed, which now feels too small. I splash some water on my face to wash the cobwebs away and make a bee-line to the only bathroom in our 978-square-feet apartment before the line starts forming. (You haven't fully lived until you're assisting one child doing a number one in the sink because your other child is taking too long doing a number two in the toilet. Had I known that was in my future, I would have gladly forked up the extra $200 a month for the two-bedroom, two-bath apartment.)

In the meantime, I pee with the door open so I can yell to everyone to wake up. Typical—the girls are going to be late for kindergarten. I dress Kiera while she is still in my bed because she's lazy in the morning and I'm a born enabler. (This must be inherited from my mom, the same woman who would bring my brother his

dinner while he was lounging in front of the TV and take his plate away.) Shayna, who wakes up to the sun shining and birds chirping, is fully dressed before I can put one sock on her sister. After they do a horrible job brushing their teeth, I put their hair in the only functional hairstyle I know: the Feather Duster (nicknamed by my sister-in-law) because I tie their bangs standing straight up and it fans out right above their foreheads. (Bangs they wouldn't have had if they hadn't decided to give each other haircuts—while mommy was on a phone interview, by the way.) I pack nutritious snacks for them that they won't eat because doing so takes away from their precious free playtime. I give them kisses, tell them I love them, and Daddy rushes them out the door to walk them to school. I breathe a sigh of relief and jump back into bed, reset my phone alarm, and wake up again to "Shake It Off."

9:00 a.m.
I jump out of bed feeling refreshed and ready to attack my day. I open the fridge and grab a small mason jar filled with my famous overnight oats and snoop around Facebook until I finish my breakfast. I take a deep breath, open my MacBook, and find more than one hundred emails from strangers seeking help. I've received email inquiries regarding weight loss, weight gain, fitness, recipes, nursing, meal planning, stretch marks, and even a few marriage proposals. I like to think of *My Healthy Dish* as my alter ego. She's the person who has more than one million followers on Instagram, travels the world for speaking appearances, partners with large corporations, and gets chased down at Disneyland for photos. Her days are the complete opposite of my day-to-day playdates, laundry, dishes, and Target runs.

12:45 p.m.
Twins are home from school. I close my computer, give the girls hugs, and march them straight to the bathroom to wash the paint and glue off their hands. They run to their room and pull out a dozen Littlest Pet Shop figurines and act out a story from *Frozen* while I prepare a quick lunch. For my little vacuum, Kiera, peanut butter and jelly and sliced apples. For my picky eater, Shayna, light on the peanut butter and jelly, no crust, and no "skin" on her apples.

1:30 p.m.
Tag, Harlen's it! My hubby gets the fun job of entertaining them and doing homework while I head back into my tiny kitchen. I finally get to do my favorite part of my job—just cooking. I rummage through my fridge and pantry until inspiration hits. (Rarely do I plan ahead with recipes.) I create a simple, healthy recipe for my blog. I plate it, photograph it, edit it, write up the recipe, and load it to all my social media channels, all the while grabbing a few bites here and there because I always forget to eat lunch.

4:00 p.m.
Snack time! My little helpers assist me while I make strawberry banana smoothies with almond milk, milled flaxseed, and honey. With a little coaxing and encouragement, I convince Shayna to finish at least half of her smoothie. I always keep an eye on her when

I feed her or else I'll find food randomly stashed around the apartment. I've actually uncovered half-eaten sandwiches wrapped in toilet paper in the garbage and baby carrots in my hamper before. Funny how I never find cookies or chips during my forced scavenger hunts. . . . We all relax as a family and unplug. All phones, computers, laptops, iPads, and televisions are shut off. I created this routine when I realized how often I reached for my phone to view other peoples' lives. When your daughters are frantically waving at you during their swim lesson and you're staring at your phone, it's time for an intervention. I gave myself a reality check to not only be physically present, but mentally present, as well.

4:30 p.m.
I toss the twins their mini iPads and make a run for it. Harlen turns on the TV and watches grown men fight over balls and stuff, and he occasionally yells at the screen. I use this time to open my Mac and get lost in photo

edits, emails, and recipe writing. Before I know it, I have to get up and make dinner. If I left dinner up to Harlen, he would be Yelping the nearest restaurant that serves wings. I take a few minutes to scroll through Facebook. Oh, how nice. I see my single friends are in Vegas again. When was the last time I saw them? Oh, well. Back to scrummaging up some dinner.

6:00 p.m.

I make a quick dinner of shrimp scampi, spring mix salad, and rice. I gently coax Shayna to eat her salad and play rock-paper-scissors with Harlen to see who will do dishes. We squeeze in a little Facetime with my parents so they can get their twin fix or else I know I'll get a phone call the next day. Then it's bath, bottle, and bed. (Bottle because they're going through a phase where they're pretending to be babies. Again, I'm an enabler because I actually took them to the store to pick out sippy cups that look like bottles.) Shayna falls asleep the moment her head hits the pillow. Her right hand is tucked beneath her body so she doesn't suck her thumb. In the meantime, Kiera leaves her room to pee, blow her nose, drink water, have a snack, and finally one of us lies with her until she falls asleep. (Wild guess which enabling parent ends up lying with her?) I tiptoe out of their room and relax in my comfy, ugly, beige recliner. I turn on my DVR—the best invention ever created—and catch up on my reality shows. Wait, who the heck is Caitlyn Jenner? When was the last time I watched TV? Apparently I have not been *Keeping Up with the Kardashians*.

10:00 p.m.

Short break into someone else's reality is over, so it's time to fold the mountain of laundry and pay bills. Wow, my credit card shows I went to Target fifteen times last month. I think that's a record for me. I then waste the next thirty minutes of my precious time searching Netflix, only to put on *Friends* and fall asleep before Ross's next divorce. When you're married with kids, there is no such thing as "Netflix and Chill"; it's only "Netflix and Pass Out." Don't feel too bad for me. By the time you read this, I should be nice and settled in my new home with two bathrooms.

SO, WHAT'S HEALTHY?

I learned pretty quickly that everyone's definition of healthy is different. Today, it's getting harder and harder to define what is actually healthy because it seems new findings will debunk previous beliefs. Eggs were once considered bad because they were believed to increase cholesterol, and now some consider them a superfood. The food pyramid we were once taught to follow in school showed almost half of our daily consumption should be from carbohydrates like bread, cereal, rice, and pasta. Now people believe it should be flipped, and that our diet should consist of mainly lean proteins, vegetables, fruit, legumes and nuts.

In addition, the popularity of MyPlate has risen because it gives us a visual of what portions should be in our plate; the pyramid only showed how many servings of each food group were recommended. Also, MyPlate shows grains as one-quarter of the plate, and vegetables and proteins as more than half. A few years ago, the Atkins Diet scared everyone away from eating carbs, now carbs are slowing making a comeback. Fairly recently, gluten has gotten a bad reputation, even though it was really the foods that accompanied gluten that were usually unhealthy and not the gluten itself. Unless you're gluten-intolerant or have Celiac disease, gluten is fine to consume. Now Genetically Modified Organisms have us worried we'll grow two heads if we eat an apple. From my understanding, GMOs are in a lot of the foods we eat. It's very difficult to avoid, especially because food manufacturers are not required to label their food as a GMO product.

Is our fish farm-raised or wild-caught? Is your chicken free-range? Is free-range really free? Is soy bad for you now? Is organic really 100 percent organic? Are we hurting the people who harvest quinoa? If the walking dead overrun the planet, will you even care if the food you scavenge is organic? Do you see the rabbit hole we're falling into?

If you look deep enough, you'll find something wrong with *everything* you eat. I don't know about you, but I don't want to feel that walking into a grocery store is like walking into a battlefield. I know I'm going to piss off a few people when I say this, but it's a lot to take in when you're just trying to figuring out what to make for dinner. This is not to say we all should be completely ignorant of the food we are buying. I believe it's important to educate ourselves and know what we are eating, but don't get to the point where you're scared to buy an apple.

I've found that it doesn't matter what type of recipe I post, I will always have some member of the food police commenting on why it's unhealthy. For a while, it was driving me nuts, trying to please everyone in fear of any negative comments. I finally had enough, though, and accepted that *my* definition of *healthy* is not going to fall in line with everyone else's. It may not be the most popular definition, but it's the most realistic and, besides, it's not like I'm going to announce I'm running for president anytime soon.

My definition of *healthy food* is real food—food that comes in as natural a state as possible, like one-ingredient foods. Foods that people living one hundred years ago would recognize that have a short shelf life, like apples, carrots, chicken, fish, rice, beans, broccoli, and so forth. That means my definition of *unhealthy foods* are processed and have multiple ingredients, are loaded in preservatives, and full of chemicals. That's how I define healthy food over unhealthy food, but, of course, there are always exceptions to the rule in both categories. So, my definition of *healthy* is sticking to real food as often as possible and indulging in *unhealthy* occasionally. Healthy is a lifestyle, not a diet. It shouldn't be full of restrictions. Food is meant to nourish and be enjoyed. I can't imagine life without chocolate chip cookies and Ruffles Cheddar Potato Chips, and I don't expect you to give up your favorite treats either. The key is to eat so much of the good stuff that you don't feel bad when you indulge in the bad stuff.

A Note About the Best Cooking Oils

Before we get to the recipes, I think it's important to talk about cooking oils. There are three oils I mainly use for everyday cooking; avocado oil, coconut oil, and olive oil. All have a different purpose, and I base their usage on their smoke points. All oils have a certain temperature they can reach before it becomes rancid. We all know that we should never burn oil; not only does it make the oil unusable, it also starts to break down and produce harmful chemicals both in the oil and in the smoke. This is why smoke points should be considered when cooking. The higher the smoke point, the safer it is to cook with at high heats. Refined versions of oils have higher smoke points. Also worth mentioning are other less popular oils like palm oil, grape seed oil, and peanut oil. They are a little more expensive and harder to find.

Avocado Oil
- *Smoke point:* 520°F
- *Health Benefits:* Avocado oil is cholesterol-free and mostly unsaturated fat. It is a great source of Vitamin E for healthy skin and eyes. Avocado oil is also high in oleic acid, which is an anti-inflammatory, can lower the risk of some cancers, and can help with cell regeneration.
- *Uses:* Great for cooking anything at high temperatures and frying. Can also be used in dressings.

Coconut Oil
- *Smoke point*: 350°F (unrefined); 450°F (refined)
- *Health Benefits:* Coconut oil contains vitamins E & K so it's great for the heart, skin, and bones. Coconut oil also has no cholesterol, but is mainly saturated fat. However, coconut oil does metabolize differently than other saturated fats, as it goes straight to the liver from the digestive tract. It can help increase energy and reduce appetite.
- *Uses:* Use coconut oil to replace butter or oil in baking recipes.

Coconut oil can also be used to sauté foods. Virgin or unrefined coconut oil will have more coconut flavor than refined oil.

Olive Oil
- *Smoke point*: 375 °F for extra virgin; 468°F for extra light
- *Health Benefits*: Extra virgin olive oil is high in antioxidants called polyphenols that can help keep the heart healthy. It is a monounsaturated fat, which means it keeps the bad cholesterol levels (LDL) down and boosts the good cholesterol, the HDL. Olive oil has zero cholesterol, is a heart-healthy choice, and contains a small amount of vitamins E and K.
- *Uses*: Olive oil is very versatile and is used in many Italian, Greek, and Spanish dishes. It's great for grilling, sautéing, roasting, drizzling, and even marinating.

Palm Oil
- *Smoke point*: 450°F
- *Health Benefits*: Palm oil is higher in Vitamin E and Vitamin A than any other plant-based oil, making it a great choice for eye health. It is also a great source of phytonutrients that can reduce the risk of diseases. Although palm oil is cholesterol-free and trans-fat-free oil, it is mainly saturated fat and should be limited like coconut oil. Make sure to use red palm oil and not palm kernel oil, as red palm oil contains more antioxidants and health benefits.
- *Uses*: Many packaged foods are replacing trans-fat oils with palm oil. Palm oil can be used for medium-heat cooking, baking, sautéing, and making dips.

Grape Seed Oil
- *Smoke point*: 475°F
- *Health Benefits*: Grape seed oil can lower blood pressure and overall heart rate. It also contains omega-6 fatty acids, which your body cannot produce, that helps with increased brain function, skin and hair growth, bone health, and metabolism.
- *Uses*: Great for cooking with high heat and can be used to replace other oils. Use grape seed oil for sautéing, roasting, and in salad dressings.

Peanut Oil
- *Smoke point*: 450°F
- *Health Benefits*: Peanut oil contains phytosterols, plant fats that are great for a healthy heart and known to lower

cholesterol and prevent cancer. This cholesterol-free oil is made of mostly heart-healthy, unsaturated fat and has small amounts of vitamins E and K.

- *Uses*: Peanut oil is used in Southern and Asian cooking. It is great for cooking with high heat. Use peanut oil for sautéing, roasting, stir-frying, deep frying, and baking.

Sesame Oil

- Smoke point: 350°F (unrefined oil); 450°F (semi-refined oil)
- Health Benefits: Sesame oil is cholesterol free and has trace amounts of vitamins E and K. It is mostly unsaturated fat so it's great for a healthy heart.
- Uses: Sesame oil is used in Asian cooking. Stir-fry with untoasted sesame oil; drizzle toasted sesame oil onto a finished dish to give it a toasty flavor and aroma or use in salad dressing.

Have you ever wondered the difference between olive oil and extra virgin olive oil? Olive oil is graded based on the production process and the acidity levels. Extra virgin olive oil is the highest quality olive oil with the best flavor. The oil is extracted by cold press and contains 1 percent acid. Virgin olive oil is made with riper olives and has an acidity of less than 2 percent. Use extra virgin olive oil for salads and dips and virgin oil for cooking.

Organic versus Nonorganic

I probably won't hear the end of it for stating this, but I don't lose sleep if I don't buy everything organic. I buy organically when it's important and affordable. If it's a real concern for you and money is an issue, at least buy organic when it comes to the "Dirty Dozen." These are the top 12 fruits and vegetables that contain the most pesticide residue. By switching these 12 to organic, you reduce your exposure to pesticide residue by 80 percent. Here is the new Environmental Working Group's 2015 "Dirty Dozen."

1. Celery
2. Peaches
3. Strawberries
4. Apples
5. Domestic blueberries
6. Nectarines
7. Sweet bell peppers
8. Spinach, kale, and collard greens
9. Cherries
10. Potatoes
11. Imported grapes
12. Lettuce

This is the list of "The Clean 15," which bore little to no traces of pesticides.

1. Onions
2. Avocados
3. Sweet corn
4. Pineapples
5. Mango
6. Sweet Peas
7. Asparagus
8. Kiwi
9. Cabbage
10. Eggplant
11. Cantaloupe
12. Watermelon
13. Grapefruit
14. Sweet potatoes
15. Sweet onions

Consider this: The misconception I come across is that healthy food is expensive, but that's not true; it just means you just need to shop smarter. Have you tried bulk bin items? Not only are you saving money buying in bulk, but you're not taking on the added cost of advertising, labeling, and packaging. You can find quinoa, lentils, rice, nuts, seeds, and dried fruit in these areas. Here's also your chance to try new things: purchase a small sample of something instead of a whole package.

WHAT'S IN MY KITCHEN?

I don't expect anyone to have a fully stocked chef's kitchen—I don't even have that. I'm giving you the basic kitchen tools to get you started and, unless you're a professional chef or a food blogger, you don't need much more than this. Don't worry—I will not make you purchase a Spiralizer. (I still don't understand what's that about.)

Recommended items include:

- Baking dish, glass
- Baking ("cookie") sheets
- Blender
- Can opener
- Casserole dish
- Cast-iron skillets: 6½-inch, 8-inch, and 10-inch
- Chef's knife, 8–9 inches
- Colander
- Cutting boards (wood for fruit and vegetables; plastic for meat)
- Foil
- Food processor
- Kitchen shears
- Ladle
- Measuring cups
- Measuring spoons
- Muffin/cupcake tray
- Nonstick pan, 10-inches
- Paring knife
- Plastic wrap
- Potato masher
- Roasting pan
- Sauce pan, 3 quarts
- Slow cooker
- Spatula
- Spice rack
- Stock pot with lid, 10 quarts
- Tongs
- Vegetable peeler
- Wax paper
- Whisk

BREAKFAST

We all know the most important meal of the day is breakfast, but do you know why? The time between dinner and breakfast is the body's longest duration without food. This, of course, means the term *breakfast* makes so much sense: you're breaking your fast. What you eat for breakfast can dictate what you eat the rest of the day. Whenever you eat, your glucose levels or blood sugar rises and your pancreas secretes insulin to convert those sugars into energy. Our bodies are always working to keep our blood levels in line. If you skip breakfast, you're pretty much running on empty with no energy to burn. Not only will you be hungry and tend to overeat, you will crave sugary foods because your blood sugar levels are low. Eating a big meal and foods high in sugar will spike your blood levels, your pancreas will go into overdrive and produce too much insulin to convert glucose into energy, and your blood sugar levels will crash, causing energy levels to lower. Once you crash, you start craving foods high in sugars to give you another jumpstart, thus starting a vicious cycle that may continue all day. Skipping breakfast can cause weight gain because of this cycle of highs and lows. I apologize—I think I'm starting to sound a lot like your mom. I don't want you to eat breakfast just to avoid putting on extra pounds. I want you to look forward to the fluffy stuffed blueberry pancakes, the warm cinnamon apple French toast casserole, or the sundried tomato and basil frittata. It would be hard for anyone to resist any of these recipes.

Stuffed Blueberry Pancakes   31

Blueberry Chia Jam   33

Vanilla Cinnamon Almond Butter   33

Baked Cinnamon Apple French Toast
    Casserole   35

Granola Baked Chicken & Waffles   36

Overnight Oats   39

Sundried Tomato & Basil Frittata   41

Spinach Mushroom Frittata   41

Banana Bread Muffins   42

Baked Avocado & Eggs   45

Sweet Potato & Chive Cakes   46

Creamy Polenta with Lemon Ricotta   47

Stuffed Blueberry Pancakes

I use to make my pancakes in a large pan, doing one or two at a time. This took forever and never came out as fluffy as when I ordered it at IHOP. I'm not sure why, but when I started using the griddle to cook pancakes, it all came out perfect. I'm perplexed on the difference between the pan and the griddle, but I swear the pancakes come out different.

1 cup whole wheat flour

½ cup oat flour

3½ teaspoons baking powder

1 egg

1 tablespoon coconut sugar

1¼ cups milk

1 teaspoon salt

3 tablespoons melted coconut oil

blueberry chia jam (see page 33)

Instructions:
Preheat griddle to 350°F or medium heat. In a large bowl, mix all ingredients except jam with a whisk. (You can also mix everything in a blender. This way, you just pour batter straight from blender onto griddle.) Spray griddle with coconut oil and pour a thin layer of batter. When it starts to slightly bubble, add a dollop of jam, spreading it out thinly. Be careful not to spread to the edges of the pancake. Add another thin layer of pancake mix on top and spread with spatula. Flip and cook for another 1½ to 2 minutes.

Blueberry Chia Jam

I once did a three-day press event for the US Highbush Blueberry Council. I stayed in Napa and was surrounded by executive chefs from all around the world who were creating delicious dishes with blueberries. Over three days, we ate and drank everything blueberry—more than you can probably imagine. I even had blueberry scented candles in my room. I thought I would eventually get tired of blueberries once I came home, but instead, I went through withdrawal. So now you can say I'm a little obsessed with this little blue dynamo.

1 tablespoon avocado oil

1 cup blueberries

2 tablespoon chia seeds

⅓ cup coconut sugar

1 tablespoon lemon juice

pinch of salt

Instructions:
In a small saucepan, heat oil and add blueberries, chia seeds, sugar, lemon juice, and salt. Smash the blueberries with spoon to release juice. Stir on medium-low heat for 10 to 15 minutes or until sauce thickens. You may store in refrigerator for up to five days and freeze up to three months.

Vanilla Cinnamon Almond Butter

I typically pack an almond butter and jelly sandwich for the girls' school lunches. You saw that I made my own blueberry jelly, so of course I had to make almond butter, as well!

1½ cups raw almonds

1 vanilla bean stick or ½ tablespoon
   vanilla extract

½ tablespoon cinnamon

½ tablespoon salt

Instructions:
Spread almonds on cookie sheet. Preheat oven to 350°F. Bake for 10 minutes, then cool for 10 minutes. Add almonds to food processor or high-quality blender. Blend until smooth, add remaining ingredients, and blend again. Please note: the almonds will stick to the sides of the blender. Turn off and use spatula to scrape the sides of blender and turn on again. You might have to repeat this process 2 to 3 times until you get your desired consistency.

Did you know *coconut oil is a saturated fat which does not contain cholesterol? Coconut oil is a blend of fatty acids—primarily lauric and myristic. Even though it's a healthier saturated fat and has the added benefits of plant-based nutrients, you should limit your intake to 7 to 10 percent of your daily calorie intake because it still can increase your risk for heart disease. Depending on room temperature, coconut oil can be solid, semi-solid, or liquid. There are many uses for coconut oil besides cooking. In the winter my coconut oil hardens to almost a wax. I use it as a natural lip balm and skin moisturizer. Some use it as toothpaste, makeup remover, and even in their hair.*

Baked Cinnamon Apple French Toast Casserole

Making a French toast casserole for the family is so much easier than standing over a pan making individual servings. It shaves off so much time during Sunday morning brunches, I get to sleep an extra twenty minutes. When you're the mommy of young twin girls, sleep always wins over hunger.

1 large red apple

3 tablespoons coconut oil or butter

2 tablespoons maple or coconut sugar

2 eggs

½ cup almond milk

¼ cup light coconut cream

1 tablespoon vanilla extract

¼ teaspoon ground cinnamon

¼ teaspoon ground nutmeg

dash of salt

8 slices sprouted grain bread

Instructions:
Preheat oven to 375°F. Cut apple, remove core, and slice into little pieces. Warm 1 tablespoon of butter on medium heat and add ½ tablespoon of sugar and chopped apples. Cook and stir until slightly brown and remove from heat. In a large bowl, add eggs, milk, cream, vanilla extract, cinnamon, nutmeg, salt, and 1 tablespoon of sugar, leaving a little sugar to sprinkle on top later. Cut up bread slices in big chunks or shred by hand. Add chunks of bread into same skillet of cooked apples. Pour mixture on top and evenly spread dollops of remaining butter. Sprinkle remaining sugar on top. Bake for 45 to 50 minutes. Serve with warm maple syrup.

Food Fact: Stevia, an FDA-approved sweetener, has become very popular in the past few years. Stevia derives from a plant, has zero calories, and is 200 times sweeter than table sugar. Stevia can replace the sugar in baking and can be added to your coffee or anything requiring sugar.

Granola Baked Chicken & Waffles

My Chicken & Waffles is a household favorite, but that wasn't always the case. The first attempt was quinoa waffles . . . and we had to feed them to my dog. As much as I am Team Quinoa, it was a bit overpowering in waffle batter. Instead, I swapped out the quinoa flour and replaced it with whole wheat flour. And here is the result!

Waffles

2 cups whole wheat flour

2 eggs

4 teaspoon baking powder

1¾ cups unsweetened almond milk

½ cup coconut oil

1 tablespoon of coconut sugar

1 teaspoon vanilla extract

¼ teaspoon salt

Baked Granola Chicken

8 pieces chicken tenderloin

½ teaspoon sea salt

½ teaspoon black pepper

2 eggs

1 cup whole wheat flour

2 cups granola

Instructions for Waffles:
Once again, I prefer to throw all these ingredients in my blender. It's a lot less work than mixing everything with a whisk. Simply pour your batter straight from the blender onto the waffle iron. (Just remember to preheat the waffle iron and spray with coconut oil before pouring batter.) Most waffle irons have a timer that tells you when to flip, even the one I got for $8 on Black Friday. Cook about 2 minutes on each side for a golden, crispy waffle.

Instructions for Baked Granola Chicken:
Preheat over 400°F. Pat chicken dry with paper towels to take away excess moisture. Season chicken with salt and pepper and beat eggs in small bowl. In three separate bowls, place beaten eggs, flour, and granola. Dip chicken in flour first and shake off any excess flour. Then dip chicken in eggs. Press chicken in granola. Really pack the granola onto the chicken with your hands to cover every inch. Spray cookie sheet with coconut oil and place the chicken onto it. Bake for 12 to 15 minutes or until golden brown.

Serve granola chicken with waffles and drizzle with warm maple syrup.

Tip: *Buy seasonal fruit and vegetables to save money. When peaches and blueberries are in season, I buy in bulk and freeze them for smoothies, make jams, and preserve them in jars.*

Overnight Oats

By far, my most popular recipe is my overnight oats. I may have not come up with the original concept, but I like to think I perfected it. Since its debut on my blog, I've noticed it has become really mainstream. I don't want to pat myself on the back, but I like to pretend I had something to do with the growing popularity of soaking oats overnight. The fact that no cooking is required makes it even more appealing. Even though it's only around 350 calories, it's surprisingly filling.

½ cup plain oats

1 cup plain almond milk, coconut milk, cashew milk, or even just milk

1 teaspoon chia seeds

1 teaspoon honey or maple syrup

dash of cinnamon

few drops of vanilla extract (if you're feeling fancy)

Instructions:
Pour all ingredients in a container, seal it up, and place in your refrigerator for at least 2 hours. I recommend using mason jars. The oats will expand to double the size and the chia seeds will turn into a gel-like consistency similar to tapioca. I prefer it cold, but you can also heat it in the microwave for 1 minute. Just because it says *overnight* oats does not mean it has to be soaked overnight and eaten for breakfast. Be a rebel and have it for lunch or dinner. Adding fruit is optional and earns you double reward points.

Do you remember Chia Pets, the clay animal figurines that sprouted grass? Now the same chia seeds used for Chia Pets are consumed all across the world as one of healthiest seeds on the planet. Unlike flaxseed, chia seeds can be digested whole; 2 tablespoons of chia seeds contain 139 calories, 4 grams of protein, 9 grams of fat, 12 grams of carbohydrates, and 11 grams of fiber, plus vitamins and minerals. It takes on a gel-like consistency in water and can replace eggs in baked goods. Add it to your smoothies, water, yogurt, and muffins. I like to start my day with a glass of warm lemon water with 1 tablespoon of chia seeds.

Tip: *Storing tomatoes in the refrigerator will break down the cell walls and make them mushy and mealy. The best place to store tomatoes is on the counter away from sunlight, single layer, not touching each other, and stem side up.*

Sundried Tomato & Basil Frittata

It's really hard to mess up this recipe, even for the dude who burns toast. Well, except for my husband. He either really can't cook or gives me food poisoning on purpose so he doesn't ever have to cook. Every time I leave on a trip, I actually prepare a few meals for the family before I leave. That's how much he doesn't cook. It's okay; I don't ever take out the garbage or fold laundry. I think that's a fair trade and the key to a successful marriage.

6 eggs

1 handful fresh basil

⅓ cup sundried tomatoes

¼ cup grated Parmesan cheese

¼ cup diced onions

½ teaspoon salt

½ teaspoon black pepper

Instructions:
Preheat oven to 375°F. In a large bowl, crack and whisk eggs. Roughly chop your basil, add to bowl along with remaining ingredients, and mix. Spray cast-iron or brush cast-iron pan with oil. Pour mixture into pan. Bake for 25 to 30 minutes.

Spinach Mushroom Frittata

Goat cheese is my secret ingredient for making my eggs creamy and savory. It also has fewer calories, lower cholesterol, and less fat than its counterpart, cow's milk cheeses.

1 tablespoon olive oil

4–5 cups spinach

6 eggs

1 cup sliced mushrooms

¼ chopped green onions

½ cup soft goat cheese

½ teaspoon salt

½ teaspoon black pepper

Instructions:
Preheat oven to 375°F. Heat ½ tablespoon olive oil on medium-low heat in a large pan and cook spinach until it wilts. Lay wilted spinach on paper towels to soak excess liquid. In a large bowl, crack and whisk eggs, add spinach, mushrooms, green onions, goat cheese, salt, and pepper. Mix all ingredients. Spray or brush cast-iron pan with oil. Pour mixture into cast-iron pan and bake for 25 to 30 minutes.

Banana Bread Muffins

The best banana bread I've ever had was from Julia's Best Banana Bread in Maui. The winding and scary drive through an off-the-beaten path to reach the shack that sold the best banana bread was well worth clinging to my seat. Since then, I've been obsessed with banana bread and have researched multiple recipes. I've developed these banana muffins through trial-and-error and they are delicious, but will always pale in comparison, in my opinion, to Julia's.

3 ripe bananas

1 cup whole wheat flour

1 cup oat flour

1 egg

½ cup applesauce

½ cup milk

2½ tablespoons honey

1 teaspoon vanilla extract

1 tablespoon coconut oil

1 teaspoon cinnamon

2 teaspoons baking powder

½ teaspoon salt

Instructions:
Preheat oven to 350°F. In a large bowl, mash bananas with a fork or potato masher. Add remaining ingredients to bowl and mix with a whisk. Spray muffin pan with oil and pour batter into molds. Bake for 20 to 25 minutes. You can also use 4-ounce Mason jars like I used instead of a muffin pan. Makes about 10 to 12 muffins.

Tip: Do not throw away overripe, spotted bananas. Overripe bananas are sweeter because the complex carbohydrates start to break down and change into simple sugars. A great way to eat overripe bananas is to add them as natural sweeteners to your smoothies or bake banana bread.

Food Fact: *More than half of the protein found in an egg is from the egg whites. It is still considered a complete protein without the yolk because it has all nine essential amino acids. Yolks have a bad reputation because they're full of cholesterol, but they also contain most of the nutrients in the egg. One egg has 186 milligrams of cholesterol, and the dietary guidelines recommend consuming less than 300 milligrams a day. New research has shown that the cholesterol in eggs does not raise blood cholesterol levels, meaning a couple of eggs a day for breakfast is okay!*

Baked Avocado & Eggs

I want to start by saying this recipe has become quite popular. In fact, you've probably seen many variations of it throughout the years. I first introduced this recipe when I started my blog. I'd never seen it before then, but now I've even seen viral YouTube videos about it. I'm just saying—how about giving your girl some credit for changing the world?

1 large avocado

2 eggs

2 tablespoons salsa

pinch of salt and pepper

Instructions:

Preheat oven to 425°F. Cut avocado in half and remove pit. With a small spoon, scoop some of the avocado flesh from the center, creating a larger crater for your eggs. Crinkle foil around each half of avocado to help it stand upright and place on cookie sheet. Separate egg whites and yolk. Evenly distribute egg whites into the craters of each avocado half. Bake for 10 minutes and remove cookie sheet from oven. Pour individual yolk into each avocado crater and bake for another 10 minutes. Cool for 15 minutes, top with salsa, and season with salt and pepper.

> *Tip:* Place unripened avocados in brown paper bag and store in dark place like your pantry. This method traps the ethylene gas they produce and helps them ripen faster. Adding a banana in the bag with the avocado will speed up the ripening process even more because it also produces ethylene gas.

Sweet Potato & Chive Cakes

The house smells so good when my sweet potato & chive cakes are cooking. I've found it works better than the aroma of coffee at getting my husband out of bed. When I want him to wash my car on Sunday mornings, I will bribe him with my cakes. I serve them up with two sunny-side-up eggs and he likes to dip the cakes in the runny yolk. I actually prefer a poached egg over the crispy cakes, but to each their own. Just writing about this one makes me hungry. It's so much better than boring old potato hash browns. I know if you make this for your family, they will be eating right out of the palm of your hand.

1 medium-sized sweet potato

1 egg

¼ cup chopped chives

2 tablespoons quinoa or wheat flour

½ teaspoon garlic powder

½ teaspoon salt

2 tablespoons coconut oil

Instructions:

Peel potato and grate it. If you don't have a grater, slice up potato into sections and add to food processor. Blend until chunky. Pour onto a paper towel and press out as much moisture as possible. Add sweet potato to a large bowl with egg, chives, flour, garlic powder, and salt. Mix well and form into 2–3-oz. flat circles about ½ inch thick. Warm up coconut oil in cast-iron skillet over medium-high heat. Cook each side of potato cake for 3 to 4 minutes or until crispy. Remove from pan and place on paper towel to soak up excess oil.

Creamy Polenta
with Lemon Ricotta

Polenta is basically cornmeal boiled into porridge. You can also bake it, fry it, and grill it. It's very versatile, just like potatoes, and can be eaten with breakfast, lunch, or dinner.

1 cup 2% milk

1 cup water

½ cup polenta

½ teaspoon salt

½ cup ricotta

1 teaspoon lemon zest

1 teaspoon lemon juice

2 tablespoons maple syrup

Instructions:

In a small saucepan, bring milk and water to a simmer. Gradually pour in the polenta and stir with a whisk to prevent clumps. Add salt and simmer for 20 to 25 minutes until polenta is soft and not gritty. You may have to stir in ¼ cup of more water during the cooking time if polenta is not soft enough. Remove from heat and let cool for 10 minutes. Mix in ricotta, lemon zest, lemon juice, and maple syrup. Serve warm.

Tip: Drink warm lemon water first thing in the morning: it stimulates your gastrointestinal tract to help absorb nutrients and help food pass. It wakes up your liver, which flushes out toxins. Lemon is an alkaline food, which helps with PH balance, and it contains pectin, a soluble fiber that aids in weight loss.

SOUPS, SIDES & SAUCES

This recipe chapter is how I view Thanksgiving. Turkey is always the main dish served during the holiday, but what I look forward to is always the food that accompanies it. Soups, sides, and sauces tie your meal together. Imagine dipping a turkey sandwich into a hot bowl of roasted cauliflower and cheddar soup on a cold winter day, grilling some steaks and slathering them with chimichurri sauce, topping your fish tacos with homemade guacamole, or digging into a mound of sweet potato salad with BBQ chicken.

Roasted Caprese Kabobs   51
Fully Loaded Baked Yams   53
Sweet Potato Salad   55
BLT Summer Rolls   57
Rosemary Garlic Purple Potatoes   58
Honey Mustard Brussels Sprouts   61
Guacamole   63
Scallop Ceviche with Grapefruit   65
Carrot Leek Soup   66
Butternut Squash Soup with Candied
   Pecans   68
Shredded Broccoli Slaw   71

Watermelon Jicama Salad with Balsamic
   Reduction   72
Chimichurri Sauce   74
Roasted Cauliflower and Cheddar Soup   75
Sausage Kale Sweet Potato Soup   76
Cauliflower Tater Tots   77
Mini Eggplant Pizza   78
Salmon Avocado Ceviche   79
Asian Collard Green Wraps   81
Baked Lemon Asparagus   83
Fruit Pizza   84

Roasted Caprese Kabobs

The traditional caprese salad is usually thick slices of tomato, thick slices of mozzarella, fresh basil, olive oil, and balsamic vinegar. Using roasted cherry tomatoes changed the entire dish. The tomatoes now have more flavor and tartness and have become the main ingredient instead of being part of an ensemble.

2 cups cherry tomatoes

2 tablespoons olive oil

2 cups mozzarella balls

big handful of basil

2 tablespoons balsamic vinegar

½ teaspoon coarse salt

Instructions:

Preheat oven to 375°F. In a large bowl, mix tomatoes and olive oil. Pour onto baking sheet. Roast tomatoes for 8 to 10 minutes. Roasting the tomatoes makes the flavor more tart, which will compliment the mildness of the cheese. Cool for 15 minutes and skewer with your cheese and basil. Drizzle with vinegar and sprinkle with salt.

Tip: When roasting vegetables you should mix them with a little oil before adding seasoning so the seasoning will stick.

Fully Loaded Baked Yams

I'm about to give you a tip that could be life-changing. No longer do you need to bake your potato in the oven for an hour. What if I told you that you could have a fully cooked baked potato in less than 5 minutes in your microwave?

1 medium-sized yam or sweet potato

⅓ cup black beans

⅓ cup corn kernels

⅓ cup chopped avocado

⅓ cup plain Greek yogurt

1 tablespoon cilantro

1 tablespoon minced red onion

dash of salt and pepper for taste

Instructions:

Wash a medium-sized potato and wrap in plastic wrap. (Make sure it's still damp when you wrap it.) Pop it in the microwave for 4½ minutes and you'll have a perfectly cooked "baked" potato when you hear the beep. Allow to cool for 10 minutes, cut in half, top with black beans, corn kernels, avocado, yogurt, cilantro, onion, salt, and pepper.

Food Fact: Iron is the most difficult mineral for the body to absorb. It is an essential mineral that plays an important role in our bodies: it helps make red blood cells, which carry oxygen around the body. Iron deficiency—anemia—can cause extreme fatigue, shortness of breath, dizziness, frequent infections, and chest pains. Foods rich in iron include red meat, pork, poultry, seafood, beans, dark leafy greens, and fortified foods. Consuming vitamin C with iron helps aid the absorption of iron. For example, try squeezing lemon juice on your steak or have it with red bell peppers. Did you know a cup of chopped red bell peppers contains three times more vitamin C than oranges?

Sweet Potato Salad

I stole this recipe from my mother-in-law. My husband says it's the best potato salad he's ever had. I, of course, had to make it my own and made it healthier by swapping out the russet potatoes with sweet potatoes and using a mayo with olive oil instead of canola, but I wouldn't dare change anything else.

2 large sweet potatoes

3 eggs

¾ cup sliced black olives

¼ cup diced red onion

⅓ cup mayo with olive oil, such as Kraft or Hellmann's

1 tablespoon olive oil

½ teaspoon onion powder

½ teaspoon garlic powder

½ teaspoon paprika

½ teaspoon salt

½ teaspoon black pepper

Instructions:
Peel sweet potatoes and cut in half. Boil for 20 minutes and drain. Boil eggs for 10 to 12 minutes and peel off shell. In a large bowl, gently break up potatoes with spoon, leaving chunks. Chop up eggs and add to bowl. Add remaining ingredients and gently mix and fold in everything with spatula. Serve!

Tip: *Washing produce in vinegar and water helps kill bacteria and reduces food contamination.*

For smooth-skin fruits and vegetables add 1 cup distilled white vinegar and 3 cups water into spray bottle. Spray entire surface of your fruit or vegetable, rub gently with hands and rinse under water. Rough or irregular surfaces require soaking in 1 cup distilled white vinegar and 3 cups water. Rub gently with hands, separate any leafy greens, and rinse under water.

BLT Summer Rolls

I purposely chose to include a recipe containing bacon because I want you to see that everything is okay in moderation. In fact, living a life with extreme restrictions does not seem healthy to me. I could have easily chosen turkey bacon because it's considered healthier, but that is false bacon in my book. Turkey bacon is actually full of nitrates and higher in sodium than regular bacon. Besides, what part of the turkey have you seen that's neon pink? If you're going to eat bacon, then eat real bacon—just make sure it's center cut and nitrate free.

8–10 slices of bacon

2 tomatoes

1 head butter lettuce

8–10 rice paper, 16 cm rounded

Mango Avocado Sauce (see below)

Mango Avocado Sauce

1 ripe avocado	1 teaspoon vinegar
1 cup mango chunks	⅓ cup avocado or
1 handful cilantro	olive oil
juice of half a lime	1 teaspoon salt

Instructions:
Blend all ingredients until smooth.

Instructions:
Preheat oven to 375°F and lay strips of bacon across cookie sheet and bake for 15 to 20 minutes. You can also fry bacon in cast-iron skillet. Remove bacon and place on paper towels to soak up excess fat. Slice tomatoes and scoop out seeds to avoid excess moisture. Wash lettuce leaves and pat dry with paper towel.

Wet rice paper in water, but do not wait until it starts to wilt. Make sure it's still firm when wet. Lay wet rice paper on cutting board; add 2 leaves of lettuce and 2 slices of tomato at the bottom. Roll and tuck once and place a strip of bacon on top. Roll and tuck again. This is to keep the tomato from getting the bacon wet. Take the right end of rice paper and fold in and do the same on the left; it should look similar to an envelope. Roll again to the very end of the rice paper. Serve with Mango Avocado Sauce.

Rosemary Garlic Purple Potatoes

The purple potato tastes like a russet potato, but it packs a more nutritious punch than its counterpart. Most white foods—white potatoes, bread, flour, sugar, rice, and pastas—lack nutrients. The more colorful your plate, the better—hence "Eat a Rainbow." Besides, isn't it prettier on a plate than boring old white potatoes?

1 lb. mini purple potatoes

½ tablespoon rosemary

1 tablespoon minced garlic

1½ tablespoon olive oil

1 teaspoon salt

1 teaspoon black pepper

Instructions:
Preheat oven to 375°F. Cut purple potatoes in half to speed up cooking time. In a casserole or baking dish, add potatoes, rosemary, garlic, olive oil, salt, and pepper. Mix and cover with foil. Bake in oven for 40 to 45 minutes.

Food Fact: The Glycemic Index ranks carbohydrates on how fast they're converted into glucose. Carbohydrates like refined sugars and breads are easier for your body to convert to glucose and shoot up blood sugar levels faster. Carbohydrates like vegetables and whole grains are digested more slowly and therefore the conversion to glucose is slower. The smaller the number, the less impact it has on blood sugar levels. Aim for 55 or less on the Glycemic Index to control blood sugar levels.

Honey Mustard Brussels Sprouts

Two things I couldn't stand when I was younger: my older brother, Le, and Brussels sprouts. Le would pick on my younger brother and me all day. One time, he even put black pepper in my brother's baby bottle. He got so many spankings from my dad, I'm pretty sure he has a permanent handprint on his butt. My feelings have since changed; he has become a very caring brother . . . or maybe I like him more because he moved a few hundred miles from us.

I was at a potluck the first time I tried Brussels sprouts. They looked so cute on the tray, almost like tiny baby cabbages. I took one bite and was instantly repulsed—it was bitter and mushy. Why in the world anyone would purposely eat them was beyond me. Now, I've changed my tune. I reluctantly tried them again because my husband asked me to make them for him. I followed a simple recipe online, and it was life changing! I've since reinvented that simple recipe and added honey and balsamic vinegar to balance some of the bitterness of Brussels sprouts. Now I'm just mad at the person who ruined Brussels sprouts for me earlier in my life. To think, I could've been eating them for the last fifteen years!

2½ cups Brussels sprouts

1½ tablespoons honey

2 teaspoons mustard powder

2 tablespoons balsamic vinegar

1½ tablespoons olive oil

½ teaspoon garlic powder

1 teaspoon salt

½ teaspoon black pepper

Instructions:
Preheat oven to 400°F. Cut Brussels sprouts in half and add to baking dish. In a small bowl, whisk the remaining ingredients and pour over Brussels sprouts. Bake in oven for 30 minutes.

Tip: I like to make extra dipping sauce for my baked Brussels sprouts. If you double up on this recipe, it makes a really delicious and light salad dressing, too. You will need: 1 tablespoon olive oil, ½ tablespoon honey, 1 tablespoon balsamic vinegar, ½ teaspoon mustard powder, and ¼ teaspoon salt.

Guacamole

People are concerned about eating avocadoes because they're high in fat, but not all fat is considered equal. Over 75 percent of fats from avocadoes are good fats—monounsaturated and polyunsaturated. Consuming good fats in moderation can actually help lower bad cholesterol.

2 large avocados

2 Roma tomatoes

½ cup chopped cilantro

¼ cup diced onions

½ teaspoon salt

½ teaspoon black pepper

Instructions:

Cut avocado in half and remove pit. With a small spoon, scoop out avocado meat into a large bowl. Dice tomatoes and add to bowl with remaining ingredients. Mix and mash with a fork until desired consistency.

Food Fact: Microgreens are what I like to call baby plants. They are miniature counterparts of full grown plants. Picked around two weeks old, they contain four to six times more nutrients than mature plants. You can find microgreens kale, radish, red cabbage, cilantro, and many more. Great for salads and in sandwiches.

Scallop Ceviche with Grapefruit

I always say don't mess with scallops because they're so naturally sweet, there's not much you need to add to them when cooking. My only exception is when I make ceviche with grapefruit. There is a perfect balance of flavors with the sweetness of the scallops and the tart bitterness of grapefruit.

1 grapefruit, segmented

⅓ cup red onion,diced

¼ cup cilantro,chopped

1 teaspoon garlic,minced

1 teaspoon apple cider vinegar

1 teaspoon salt

½ teaspoon black pepper

6–8 colossal scallops

juice of 3 limes

Instructions:
In a large bowl, add grapefruit, onion, cilantro, garlic, vinegar, salt, and pepper. Thinly slice scallops into about 4 sections and add to bowl with lime juice. Mix all ingredients and cover with plastic wrap. Place in refrigerator for 1 hour. Serve with your favorite tortilla chips.

Carrot Leek Soup

The number-one excuse I hear about why we don't eat healthy is because there's not enough time to do so. I get it, guys! (There have been a few blurry days where I had to remind myself to brush my teeth.) Vegetable soup is one of those time-saving meals, though. It literally takes less than 30 minutes from start to finish. My trick is to cut my vegetables really small before boiling to shave off cooking time. I even sometimes double up on this recipe and freeze the rest in freezer bags.

6–8 large carrots

2 garlic cloves

1 leek stalk

2 tablespoons olive oil

1 tablespoon turmeric

1 tablespoon sea salt

2 cups vegetable stock

4 cups water

2 tablespoons plain yogurt

Instructions:
Thinly slice carrots and garlic. Cut root of leeks and most of the green stem. The more you keep of the green, the tougher it is to chew. Slice the stalk lengthwise and chop. Place the chopped pieces in a large bowl of water to remove dirt. Drain and place on paper towel. In a large pot, heat oil to medium and add carrots, leeks, and garlic. Cook for 4 to 5 minutes and add the remaining ingredients, except yogurt, to the pot. Bring your heat to high and boil for 10 minutes. Let cool for 5 to 10 minutes and purée in your blender with yogurt.

Butternut Squash Soup with Candied Pecans

My butternut squash soup with candied pecans tastes just like the holidays in a bowl. It's creamy, savory, and sweet. A perfect quick meal for the family to scarf up before the mad dash to open presents.

For soup:

1 medium-sized butternut squash

¼ onion

2 garlic cloves

3 tablespoons olive oil

2 cups vegetable stock

½ teaspoon cinnamon

1 tablespoon salt

For candied pecans:

1 tablespoon coconut oil

1 cup raw pecans

1 tablespoon maple syrup

1 tablespoon coconut sugar

¼ teaspoon cinnamon

Instructions:

Peel butternut squash, cut in half, and slice into 1½-inch pieces. Lay butternut squash, onion, and garlic cloves onto cookie sheet and brush with 1 tablespoon of olive oil. Preheat oven to 400°F degrees and bake for 25 to 30 minutes. Cool for 15 minutes and blend in food processor or blender with 2 cups vegetable stock. Pour into a large pot and stir in rest of olive oil, cinnamon, and salt. Reheat on low heat for another 5 minutes.

In a small saucepan on medium-low heat, add the coconut oil and pecans. Cook for 2 to 3 minutes while stirring pecans around. Lower heat to low and add maple syrup, coconut sugar, and salt and cook for another 3 to 4 minutes, continuously stirring so the sugar does not burn. Turn off heat and sprinkle with cinnamon. Top candied pecans on your butternut squash soup.

Tip: Butternut squash is really tough to cut. To soften, I suggest microwaving for 5 minutes before cutting into it. Or you can make life a lot easier on yourself and buy your squash precut.

Shredded Broccoli Slaw

I swear it takes us an hour to decide where to go for dinner sometimes. The four of us rarely ever agree on what food we want to eat. It's also very tricky because Shayna is my little picky eater. The only place we can ever go that makes everyone happy is Sweet Tomato because there are so many choices. It has a salad bar, a variety of soups, breads, pizza, and pastas. I always pile the broccoli salad high on my plate. I'm 100 percent sure it's not healthy because it's full of mayo and sugar, but it's hard to resist. I think my own version, using shredded stems, is just as good, but a lot healthier. I used coconut cream instead of mayo for a similar creamy texture, but if you don't have it, just skip it.

2 tablespoons honey

2 tablespoons Dijon mustard

⅓ cup lite coconut cream

2 tablespoons olive oil

2 tablespoons apple cider vinegar

½ tablespoon minced garlic

½ teaspoon salt

½ teaspoon black pepper

1 (12-oz.) bag of shredded broccoli
   stems mix

⅓ cup dried cranberries

⅓ cup shelled sunflower seeds

1 tablespoon coconut sugar

1 chopped green apple (optional)

Instructions:
In a large bowl, add honey, Dijon mustard, coconut cream, olive oil, vinegar, garlic, salt, and pepper. Whisk really well and add remaining ingredients. Mix until sauce is evenly distributed.

Watermelon Jicama Salad with Balsamic Reduction

I don't think people appreciate Jicama like I do. It's the ugly brown root you pass by at the grocery store never giving it much thought. Don't judge a book by its cover—inside the layer of brown skin is a white root that is mildly sweet. It's the perfect way to add crunch to a salad (instead of the stale bread you call croutons). It's also high in fiber and rich in potassium, calcium, and magnesium.

1 Jicama root

1 mini watermelon

¼ cup chopped mint

½ cup feta cheese crumbles

½ teaspoon salt

½ cup balsamic vinegar

Instructions:
Peel outer layer of jicama root and cut interior into small, bite-sized cubes. Cut and cube watermelon as well. In a large bowl, add watermelon, jicama, mint, feta cheese, and salt. In small saucepan, simmer balsamic vinegar until it reduces to half and drizzle over salad.

Chimichurri Sauce

Please be advised, you will become addicted to my Chimichurri sauce, so make it at your own risk—and make a big batch. The sauce goes fast in my house. We put it on our steak, chicken, fish, eggs, tacos, and we even dip our bread in it. I've even used it for salad dressing.

1 cup parsley

½ cup cilantro

5 cloves garlic

⅓ onion

⅓ cup apple cider vinegar

⅓ cup olive oil

½ tablespoon salt

1 teaspoon black pepper

Instructions:
Blend in food processor or blender and store in refrigerator until ready to eat.

> ***Tip:*** Replace your spices once a year. Over time, spices and dried herbs lose flavor. Rub your spices between your fingers. If it has a faint aroma then it has lost most of its flavor. Another indicator that flavor is gone is if the color fades.

Roasted Cauliflower and Cheddar Soup

Have you heard of umami? The basic four taste flavors were sweet, salty, sour, and bitter. Just recently, umami has been added as a fifth taste. It's hard to describe, but how do you describe any of the other tastes? Some say it's a pleasant, savory taste. Think fatty meats or cheeses. When I have a spoonful of my roasted cauliflower and cheddar soup, the best way for me to describe the taste or experience is *umami*. Or maybe it's all the flavors wrapped into one . . . Who really knows? This idea is open to each person's experience and interpretation.

1 head cauliflower

2 tablespoons olive oil

2 cloves garlic

½ onion, chopped

1 cup vegetable broth

½ tablespoon butter

½ cup coconut cream

1 teaspoon black pepper

1 teaspoon salt

1 cup cheddar cheese, shredded

Instructions:
Preheat oven to 400°F. Cut cauliflower into florets and place on baking sheet. Drizzle 1 tablespoon oil over cauliflower and bake in the oven for 18 to 20 minutes. In a large pan, heat 1 tablespoon olive oil to medium heat and sauté whole garlic and chopped onions until onions are translucent. Add broth, butter, coconut cream, salt, and pepper. Simmer for 10 minutes and turn off heat. Add cheese and stir until it melts. Pour soup into blender with roasted cauliflower and blend to desired consistency. Pour in serving bowls when ready to eat and sprinkle with a little sprinkle of more cheese.

Sausage Kale Sweet Potato Soup

This is a stick-to-your-ribs kind of hearty meal. One big bowl and I'm ready to snuggle on the couch and take a nap. This recipe is proof positive that healthy food can be filling and satisfying at the same time.

1 tablespoon garlic, minced

½ onion, diced

1 pound Italian turkey sausage, casing removed

2 sweet potatoes, peeled and roughly chopped

1 (8-oz.) can cannellini beans

4 cups vegetable stock

2 tablespoons olive oil

1 teaspoon dried oregano

1 teaspoon salt

1 teaspoon black pepper

3 cups kale, chopped

Instructions:
In a large pot, warm oil to medium heat and add garlic and onions. Cook for 2 to 3 minutes. Add turkey sausage and, with a large spoon, break up pieces while cooking. Add remaining ingredients, except kale, and simmer for 20 minutes. Add kale last and cook for another 5 minutes.

> **Tip:** I know it's odd to say, but you should massage kale if you plan on eating it in your salads. Kale is a little coarser and rougher and I often use it more for soups and sautés. For using kale in salads it's best to massage it with a little olive oil or salad dressing for 2 to 3 minutes to break down cellulose structure and soften.

Cauliflower Tater Tots

I swear, if you made these for the family and didn't tell them it was cauliflower, they wouldn't even know the difference from normal tots. If only school cafeterias would switch to my recipe. Imagine how many happy parents there would be. Hey, if my picky eater Shayna eats these, then any kid will love them.

1 medium head cauliflower, trimmed and cut into florets

⅓ cup quinoa flour

¾ cup panko crumbs

½ cup Parmesan, grated

½ teaspoon baking powder

¼ teaspoon salt

¾ teaspoon black pepper

2 egg whites or 1 whole egg

2½ tablespoons avocado oil

Instructions:

Preheat oven to 400°F. Boil cauliflower in a large pot for 10 minutes or until fork-tender and drain. Blend in food processor or blender to a chunky consistency. Pour over center of cheesecloth or dishtowel. Strain cauliflower through cloth to remove as much moisture as possible and add to large bowl with quinoa flour, panko crumbs, Parmesan, baking powder, salt, and pepper. Mix everything and form 1-oz.-size tots with hands. Line a baking sheet with wax paper or foil and brush with oil. Place tots onto sheet and brush each one with oil. Bake for 18 to 20 minutes.

Mini Eggplant Pizza

No, it's not delivery, and it's not Digiorno either. It's a healthier, cheaper pizza you can make at home. It may not be your traditional pizza, but why not try a twist on a classic? I do this with thick zucchini slices, too, and it's a hit with my family and friends!

1 large eggplant

⅓ cup olive oil

1 (15-oz.) can organic tomato sauce

1 tablespoon dried oregano

1 tablespoon salt

1 tablespoon black pepper

½ cup grated Parmesan

1½ cups shredded mozzarella

1 handful fresh basil

Instructions:
Preheat oven to 350°F. Cut eggplant into ½-inch thick slices. Brush each side with olive oil and spread slices on cookie sheet lined with foil. Add spoonful of tomato sauce and spread it around. Sprinkle with oregano, salt, and pepper. Top with Parmesan and mozzarella. Brush the basil leaves with a little olive oil to avoid burning and lay across cheese. Bake for 15 to 20 minutes.

Salmon Avocado Ceviche

Ceviche is typically made with raw fish and cured in citrus juice. I used to think it was raw, but the acidity from the lime juice cooks the fish. It's often served as appetizer. I recommend eating it with blue corn tortilla chips. Don't limit yourself to just salmon; also try scallops, shrimp, snapper, clams, and even lobster.

6–8 oz. skinless salmon fillets

1 avocado

1 tomato

½ onion

1 jalapeño

½ tablespoon apple cider vinegar

1 teaspoon salt

1 teaspoon black pepper

3 limes

Instructions:

Cut salmon in small chunks. Dice avocado, tomato, onion, and jalapeño. Put salmon, avocado, tomato, onion, and jalapeño, vinegar, salt, and pepper in a large bowl. Squeeze juice from limes into bowl and mix. Cover bowl with plastic wrap and place in refrigerator for at least 30 minutes to cure before eating.

Asian Collard Green Wraps

When I made this recipe I ran out of collard green leaves before I finished with my ground turkey filling. The leftovers of the ground turkey I used the next day with brown rice and an over-easy egg for breakfast. It was so delicious with the rice that now I make a little extra just so I can have it for breakfast the next day. If you make this recipe, be sure to try it with rice also.

1 tablespoon sesame oil

1 tablespoon garlic, minced

1 pound lean ground turkey

1 (8-oz.) can water chestnuts, roughly chopped

⅔ cup green onion, chopped

2 tablespoons hoisin sauce

1 teaspoon soy sauce

1 tablespoon honey

1 tablespoon lemongrass paste

juice of half a lime

½ teaspoon chili flakes (optional)

½ teaspoon salt

½ teaspoon black pepper

1 bunch of collard greens

½ tablespoon sesame seeds

Instructions:

Heat a large, nonstick pan to medium and add oil and garlic. Cook for 1 minute or until garlic turns slightly brown and then add turkey. Cook and stir around for 5 to 6 minutes, chop water chestnuts, and add to pan. Cook for another minute and add green onion, hoisin sauce, soy sauce, honey, lemongrass, lime juice, chili flakes, salt, and pepper. Cook and stir all the ingredients for another 5 to 6 minutes or until turkey is fully cooked. Sprinkle sesame seeds on top and let cool for 15 minutes. Wash collard green leaves and wipe dry with paper towel. Scoop up about 1 to 2 ounces of ground turkey filling onto middle of collard leaf and spread evenly up and down, leaving one inch on top and bottom. Wrap both sides around filling like a taco or wrap. Repeat with each leaf.

Baked Lemon Asparagus

Parmesan cheese is a bit salty so if you want to skip the salt in this recipe you can add ¼ cup more cheese. When the cheese bakes and melts it turns crispy and crunchy. The contrast goes perfectly with the tender asparagus. When choosing your asparagus make sure it's firm and not bendable, the color is a bright green, and the tips of the asparagus should be closed tightly.

1 pound of asparagus spears

2 tablespoons olive oil

juice of half a lemon

½ teaspoon garlic powder

½ teaspoon salt

½ teaspoon black pepper

zest of whole lemon

⅓ cup shaved Parmesan

Instructions:

Pre-heat oven to 375°F. Spread asparagus onto cooking sheet. Brush olive oil and lemon juice all over asparagus, season with garlic powder, salt, and pepper. Top with shaved Parmesan. Bake for 8 to 10 minutes. Remove from oven and sprinkle with lemon zest.

> *Tip:* Instead of cutting off the hardened ends of asparagus, try just cutting the tip off and using a potato peeler for the rest. You waste less asparagus and get more bang for your buck.

Fruit Pizza

A fun way to get kids involved in the kitchen and eat more fruit is making fruit pizzas. I toast Naan bread, have the girls spread soft goat cheese, and top with their favorite fruits. This time we used sliced kiwi and added slivered almonds for a little crunch. Depending on the season sometimes fruit can be a bit sour, especially kiwi. Our trick to add a little more sweetness to our fruit pizza is to drizzle a little honey on top of our goat cheese before adding fruit.

LUNCH & DINNER

You ever wonder why you can combine breakfast and lunch and call it brunch, but we don't have Dunch? Be a trend setter; try one of my many dunch recipes for your next early dinner or late lunch.

Baked Vegetarian Taco Bowls   86
Orange Ginger Salmon with Crispy
    Quinoa Salad   89
Pineapple Shrimp Wild Rice   91
Shrimp and Garlic Noodles   92
Lemon Herb Chicken with Roasted Red
    Pepper Purée   95
Korean Glass Noodles   96
Tofu Veggie Stir Fry   99
Fish & Kale Chips   101
Kale Basil Pesto   102
Sticky Red Chicken   105
Grilled Basil Shrimp Scampi 106
Stuffed Quinoa Bell Peppers   107
Mexican Lasagna   108

Teriyaki Mahi Mahi Pineapple Kabobs   109
Buffalo Tofu Sticks   110
Vegan Alfredo Sauce with Roasted
    Tomatoes and Mushrooms   111
Vegan Burger   112
Creamy Butternut Squash Mac & Cheese
    114
Cheesy Turkey Meatballs   117
Marinara with Brown Rice Pasta   119
Broccoli Cheese Quesadilla   120
Avocado on Toast   121
Chickpea Greek Salad   123
Steak Fajita Salad Bowl   125
Shrimp Scampi Tacos with Mango
    Avocado Salsa   127

Baked Vegetarian Taco Bowls

The number one concern when making vegetarian or vegan dishes is protein. Will there be enough? Well, you will be surprised to learn that 1 serving of lentils has 12 grams of protein. To put that in perspective, 1 egg has 6 grams of protein. Even though I heard some huffing and puffing from my hubby, the caveman, the swap from ground beef to lentils was relatively easy for Kiera and me. Shayna wouldn't even try it, but with a picky eater, I can't win them all.

½ cup uncooked lentils

1 tablespoon small packet of taco seasoning

1 teaspoon salt

1 teaspoon black pepper

8 small corn tortilla tacos

2 tablespoons avocado oil

½ cup cheddar cheese, shredded

½ cup plain Greek yogurt

1 tomato

1 avocado

Instructions:
Add lentils and 2 cups water to a saucepan, bring to boil, and reduce heat to low. Cover with lid and simmer for 25 to 30 minutes. Drain excess water and mix in taco seasoning, salt, and pepper. Preheat oven to 350°F. Stack 4 tortillas in a damp paper towel and heat in microwave for 30 seconds. The moisture will make it easy to bend the tortilla without breaking it. Brush each side with avocado oil. Flip your muffin tray upside down and insert each tortilla in the crevices, creating a bowl. Bake for 10 minutes or until golden brown. Add your cooked lentils, shredded cheese, yogurt, chopped tomatoes, and avocado.

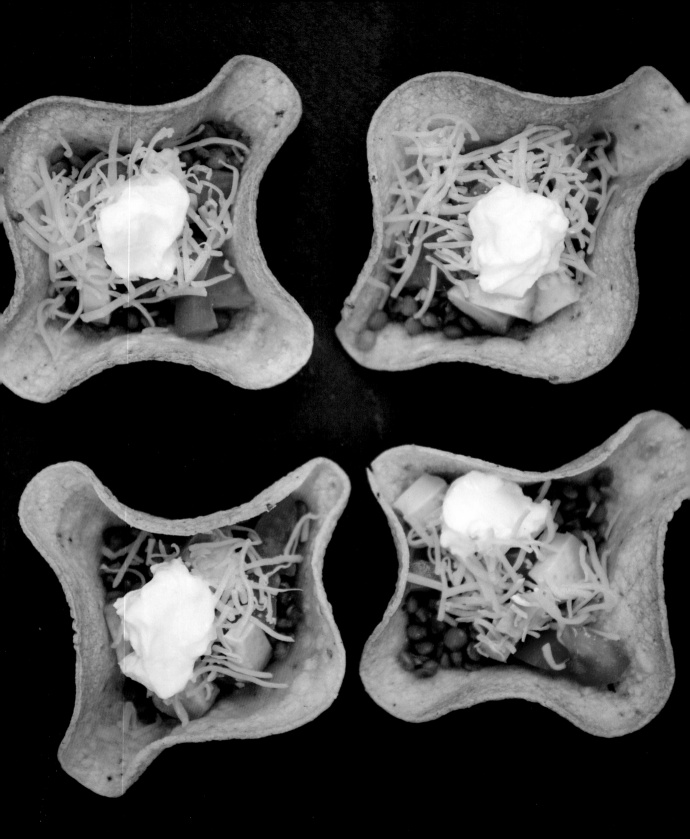

Orange Ginger Salmon with Crispy Quinoa Salad

I know this picture may look intimidating to the amateur chef, but it's actually one of my more cooking-for-dummies recipes. My mother-in-law loves my salmon and says it melts like butter when you bite into it. In fact, she insists I invite her over every time I make it.

Salmon Marinade:
3–4 (6–8-oz.) salmon fillets
juice of 2 oranges or ½ cup of orange juice
    (but fresh is always best in my book)
2 oz. fresh sliced ginger or
    1½ tablespoon ginger paste
1 tablespoon garlic, crushed
1 tablespoon maple syrup
¼ cup low-sodium soy sauce
¼ cup apple cider vinegar
¼ cup avocado oil
avocado oil spray or olive oil spray
½ teaspoon salt
½ teaspoon black pepper
10 oz. clamshell of spring mix salad
2 oranges, sliced

Instructions:
Preheat oven to 350°F. Add all ingredients in a large Ziploc bag and marinate 2 hours in refrigerator. In a large baking dish, spray avocado oil, place salmon skin-down, and pour remaining marinade from bag. Bake salmon for 20 to 25 minutes. The marinade will caramelize to a brown glaze from the sugars of the syrup and orange juice. Brush the glaze over the top of salmon for a richer flavor.

Crispy Quinoa

If you've never cooked quinoa, it's just like cooking rice: 1 part quinoa to 2 parts water. So, for 1 cup quinoa, add 2 cups water. In small saucepan, bring to a boil and then simmer for 12 minutes.

Bring it up a notch and fry your quinoa in avocado oil for a crispy, nuttier flavor. Add 1 tablespoon of avocado oil per ½ cup of cooked quinoa in a pan over medium heat for 2 to 3 minutes. Toss in your salad, cut up some sliced oranges, and drizzle the leftover glaze from your salmon pan.

Pineapple Shrimp Wild Rice

My mom told me that, before I moved anything into my new house, I had to bring in a bag of rice and fish sauce first. She said it represents bringing fortune into your home. It may sound like an old wives' tale, but she's been right on ridiculous things before. Throughout my pregnancy, my mom warned me to drink only warm water after my delivery or else I would be forever cold. She even harassed all the nurses coming into my room about it. Well, I didn't listen, and now I sleep with two blankets. The moral of this story: make this recipe. It has rice and, therefore, will bring you good fortune. (I'll save the story about eating pig feet soup to produce more breast milk for my next book.)

2 tablespoons sesame or avocado oil

1 tablespoon garlic, crushed

1½–2 lb. shrimp, peeled and deveined

½ cup yellow onions, chopped

½ cup green onions, sliced

1 cup frozen mixed vegetables, soaked in hot water and drained

1 cup pineapple, diced

2 eggs

2 cups wild, brown, or white rice, cooked

2 tablespoons low-sodium soy sauce

¼ teaspoon salt

¼ teaspoon black pepper

Instructions:

Get all your ingredients lined up because this is all about timing and it moves fast. In a large pan, warm oil over medium heat. Add garlic and yellow onions and stir for 1 minute. Add green onions and shrimp and stir gently for 2 minutes. Add in mixed vegetables and pineapple for 1 minute. Add 2 eggs and scramble in pan slightly, then add rice. Add soy sauce, salt, and pepper, and mix everything gently. If you have any leftover juice from cutting your pineapple, throw that in, too!

Shrimp and Garlic Noodles

I actually stole this recipe from my little brother. It's a menu favorite at his restaurant, Blue Saigon, located in Pittsburg, California. #ShamelessPlug. Don't worry, my version is way healthier and a lot easier to make.

1 box quinoa pasta (I used Ancient Grain Pasta)

2 tablespoons sesame or avocado oil

3 tablespoons garlic, minced

2 lb. shrimp (you may peel shell, but I chose to leave it on for the sake of a pretty photo and sticky fingers)

2 tablespoons oyster sauce

2 tablespoons maple syrup

juice of half a lemon

½ teaspoon salt

½ teaspoon black pepper

Instructions:

Follow instructions on box to boil pasta. Do not boil longer than 8 minutes or it will stick and be too soft. Drain and rinse under cool water to stop cooking and prevent sticking. In a large pan, warm oil over medium heat and add garlic. Cook until garlic is light brown and then add shrimp. Cook for 1½ minutes on each side and reduce heat to low. Add noodles, oyster sauce, maple syrup, lemon juice, salt, and pepper. With tongs or chopsticks, carefully mix everything until sauce is evenly spread, keeping on low heat for another 3 to 4 minutes. I added arugula for a peppery bite at the very end and to avoid wilting.

Food Fact: You can find quinoa pasta almost anywhere. I've seen it at Safeway, Target, Costco, Whole Foods, Sprouts, and Trader Joe's. If you can't find it in a store near you, check online.

My trick to choosing correct portion sizes:

A serving of steak or chicken is 3 ounces, which is about the size of a deck of cards.

A serving of fish is 3 ounces, which is about the size of a checkbook.

A serving of vegetables is ½ cup, about the size of a light bulb.

A serving size of whole fruit is about the size of a tennis ball; cut-up fruit is the size of 7 cotton balls.

Lemon Herb Chicken with Roasted Red Pepper Purée

Sometimes you just want the natural flavor of the food to speak for itself. The sweet savory red pepper purée is so delicious that I didn't think it was necessary to season my lemon herb chicken. The purée works as a sauce to compliment the chicken. With each bite, I recommend drenching it in the sauce.

Lemon Herb Chicken:

3 skinless chicken breast fillets

½ teaspoon garlic powder

½ teaspoon salt

½ teaspoon black pepper

3 slices lemon

3 sprigs rosemary

1½ tablespoons avocado oil

Roasted Red Pepper Purée:

2 red bell peppers

1 tablespoon olive oil

½ tablespoon lime juice

3 tablespoons light sour cream

1 teaspoon salt

For Chicken:

Preheat oven to 400°F. Hold knife against side of chicken and press your hand on top, cutting chicken with a sawing motion. Be careful not to cut all the way through. Fold out the chicken and season both sides with garlic powder, salt, and pepper. Place sliced lemon and sprig of rosemary on one side of butterfly chicken and fold other side on top. Warm oil over medium-high heat in cast-iron skillet. Sear chicken on both sides for 1 to 2 minutes and finish cooking in the oven for 18 to 20 minutes.

For Purée

Preheat oven to 400°F. Roast bell peppers over direct flame on stovetop until outer skin blisters and slightly blackens. Watch carefully and rotate sides to cook all around. Line cookie sheet with wax paper and place blistered bell peppers on top. (If you have an electric oven, you can add an additional 5 minutes to your baking time.) Bake for 10 minutes and cool for 10 minutes. Under running water, peel skin off pepper, remove stem and seeds. Add to blender with oil, lime juice, sour cream, and salt. Blend until smooth.

Korean Glass Noodles

The traditional Korean Glass Noodle dish usually has sliced steak, but I opted not to include it because I wanted to show you how simple it is to make many dishes vegan. The sliced Shitake mushrooms give you such a meaty texture, you won't even miss the steak.

8 oz. or 1 bundle of uncooked Korean sweet potato starch noodles (also known as Dangmyeon)

4 tablespoons low-sodium soy sauce

1 tablespoon of maple syrup

½ teaspoon salt

½ black pepper

1 tablespoon sesame oil

1 tablespoon minced garlic

2 red bell peppers, sliced

2 cups shitake mushrooms, sliced

1 teaspoon sesame seeds

4–5 green onion stalks, sliced into 1½-inch pieces

Instructions:
In a large pot, boil water. Once water starts to boil, add your noodles for 7 to 8 minutes. You want your noodles chewy, not mushy. Drain and rinse in cold water. In a small bowl, whisk soy sauce, maple syrup, salt, and pepper. In a large, nonstick pan, warm sesame oil over medium heat, add garlic, bell peppers, and green onions. Cook for 2 minutes and add your mushrooms then cook for another 2 minutes. Add your noodles and sauce to pan and stir gently until ingredients are mixed together and noodles are reheated. Top with sesame seeds.

Tofu Veggie Stir Fry

Tofu has a very soft and silky texture, mild flavor, and is very popular in Asian cuisine and popular with vegetarians. Everyone says the same thing about tofu: it doesn't taste like much so it takes on any flavor you add to it. One thing people forget to tell you, though, is that it's pretty much one of the easiest things to make. It's really hard to overcook or burn. I once heard a chef say, "You just cook the hell out of it until you think it's done."

2 tablespoons avocado oil

1 (14-oz.) container extra-firm tofu

1 pound thin asparagus spears

1½ tablespoon sesame oil

1 tablespoon garlic, minced

½ tablespoon lemongrass paste

6–8 ounces Shitake mushrooms

1 tablespoon low-sodium soy sauce

1 tablespoon oyster sauce

½ tablespoon honey

½ teaspoon salt

½ teaspoon black pepper

Instructions:

Heat avocado oil in a large, nonstick pan on medium. Slice tofu into five sections. Press a paper towel over the tofu to soak up excess liquid. Fry tofu on each side for 8 to 10 minutes or until crispy and then place on cutting board. Press another paper towel on the crispy tofu to soak up excess oil. Cut tofu into large, bite-sized pieces and set aside.

In a large, nonstick pan, add ⅓ cup water, bring to a simmer, and then add asparagus. The asparagus will start cooking in the hot water, but the water will evaporate within 3 to 4 minutes. Once all water evaporates, add sesame oil, garlic, and lemongrass paste and cook for another minute. Turn heat to medium, add mushrooms, and cook for 2 to 3 minutes, stirring occasionally. Finally, mix in tofu, oyster sauce, honey, salt, and pepper and cook for another 2 to 3 minutes. You can serve this as is or have it with a side of brown rice or quinoa.

Fish & Kale Chips

Fried fish in a healthy cookbook . . . I must not know what I'm doing, right? I'm comparing this dish to typical fish & chips you would order. You know, the one that comes in a greasy brown paper bag with a side of fried potatoes? I used avocado oil (which is one of the healthiest oils you can eat), cod (a lean fish), whole wheat flour, and panko crumbs. I also paired my fish with baked kale chips instead of fried potatoes.

Fried Fish Sticks:

1 pound cod fillets

1 cup whole wheat flour

½ teaspoon garlic powder

½ teaspoon onion powder

½ teaspoon salt

½ teaspoon black pepper

2 eggs

1½ cups panko crumbs

2 teaspoons apple cider vinegar

1 cup avocado oil

Salt & Vinegar Kale Chips:

2 cups shredded kale

2 tablespoons avocado oil

¼ teaspoon salt

For Fish Sticks:

Cut cod fillets in half diagonally down to 2-oz. pieces. In a small bowl, mix wheat flour, garlic powder, onion powder, salt, and pepper. Whisk eggs in another small bowl and place panko crumbs in another bowl. Dip fish into flour mixture first and shake off, then dip into egg mixture, and then into panko crumbs. In cast-iron pan, warm oil over medium-high heat and fry fish sticks 2 to 3 minutes on each side or until golden brown. Place on paper towels to soak up excess oil.

For Kale Chips:

Preheat oven to 350°F. Cut kale leaves from stem into bite-sized pieces. In a large bowl, add your kale, vinegar, oil, and salt. Mix gently so ingredients spread evenly. Spray cookie sheet with oil and spread kale. Add to oven immediately before vinegar wilts the kale. Bake for 10 minutes.

Kale Basil Pesto

Oh, Kale, I remember when you were just a garnish served at restaurants and discarded like trash. Now you're so popular, Michelin-star restaurants are charging $20 to serve you as a side. Oh, how times have changed.

⅓ cup pine nuts

1 cup kale without stems

1 handful fresh basil

⅓ cup olive oil

1 garlic clove

½ tablespoon lime juice

1 teaspoon lemon zest

1 teaspoon salt

½ teaspoon black pepper

3 oz. Parmesan cheese

1 bag brown rice pasta fusilli

Instructions:
Warm a nonstick pan over medium-low heat. Add pine nuts and toast, mixing around with a large spoon to avoid burning. Toast for 3 to 4 minutes or until golden brown. Add toasted pine nuts and remaining ingredients to food processor or blender. Mix until creamy. In a large pot, bring water to boil, add pasta, cook uncovered for 7 to 10 minutes, stirring occasionally to avoid clumping together. Drain pasta in colander. In a large bowl, add cooked pasta and kale pesto sauce, gently mix and fold with a spoon until sauce is evenly distributed. This dish can be served hot or cold.

Tip: Wrap paper towels around your greens when storing them to absorb moisture and keep them fresher longer. I do this with a lot of my leafy greens and herbs like kale, spinach, cilantro, and parsley. Replace paper towels every other day.

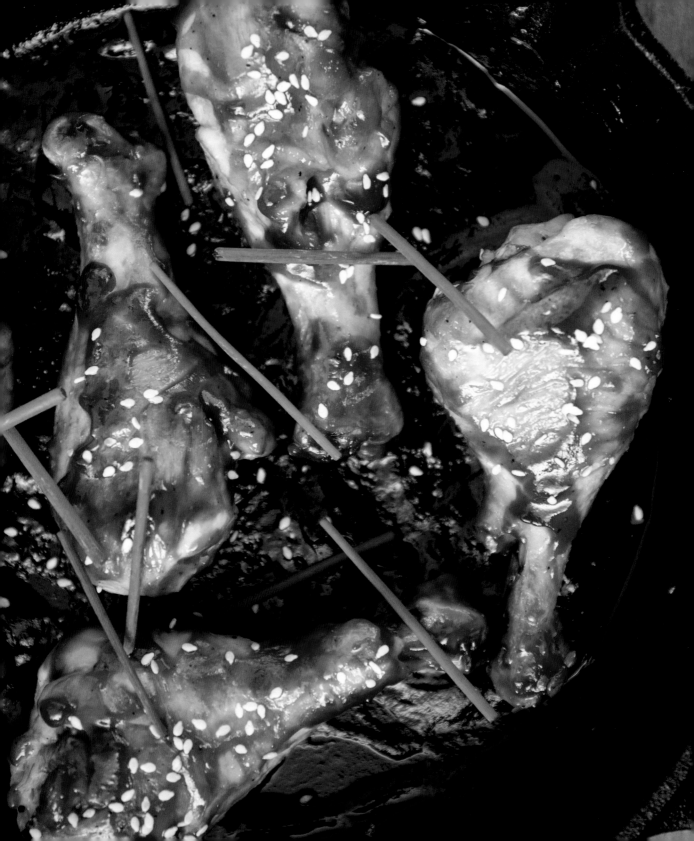

Sticky Red Chicken

This is a recipe I stole from my dad, but of course I had to make it a bit healthier. It's one that is requested over and over when family visits. He serves it over a bed of lettuce, tomatoes, and sliced boiled eggs. It's best with a big bowl of steaming rice to soak up all the sauce from the chicken. My mouth is literally watering just thinking about it. Honestly, you never truly appreciate home cooking until you move away from home. My version is good, but it will never compare to my dad's.

1½ tablespoons avocado oil

5–6 chicken drumsticks

1 teaspoon salt

⅓ cup ketchup

1 tablespoon hoisin sauce

1 tablespoon soy sauce

juice of half a lime

¼ teaspoon garlic powder

½ tablespoon coconut sugar

¼ teaspoon black pepper

Instructions:
Preheat oven to 400°F. Warm oil over medium-high heat in 10-inch cast-iron. Season chicken with ½ teaspoon salt and sear on both sides for 3 to 4 minutes. Bake for 15 to 20 minutes. In a small bowl, mix the remaining ingredients for sauce. Remove chicken from pan and pour out most of the oil and fat drippings, leaving a little to simmer the sauce. Reheat the pan over low heat and add sauce. Stir until sauce thickens and bubbles. Add back in and cook in sauce for another 2 minutes. Sauce should coat the chicken.

Food Fact: Is soy unhealthy? Soy contains isoflavones, natural plant chemicals that bind to estrogen receptors and can have similar effects as estrogen, but human estrogen is more than one thousand times stronger. The concern is that consuming too much soy can increase the risk of cancer, but Asian populations that consume the most soy products actually have lower rates of breast cancer. Isoflavones also help regulate cell growth and cholesterol levels. It is also a good source of plant-based protein and fiber compared to animal protein, which contains cholesterol. There are many cons when it comes to eating soy products, but I still believe the good outweighs the bad on this.

Grilled Basil Shrimp Scampi

I know this is contradictory, but one time I had my basil shrimp scampi with my vegan alfredo sauce and it was amazing! Hands down, one of the best meals I've made. It wasn't intentional; I just had leftover alfredo from the night before when I made the shrimp. You don't have to try it together because the shrimp is delicious on its own, but I do recommend pairing it with the alfredo at least once. I promise you won't be disappointed.

1½–2 pounds shrimp, peeled and deveined

2 tablespoons olive oil

⅓ cup basil

2 tablespoons garlic, minced

½ teaspoon onion powder

1 teaspoon salt

1 teaspoon black pepper

juice of one half a lemon

½ tablespoon Worcestershire sauce

dozen wooden skewers

Instructions:

In a large freezer bag, place shrimp, oil, basil (save a dash to sprinkle on top cooked shrimp), garlic, onion powder, Worcestershire, salt, and pepper. Zip bag, shake ingredients, and place in refrigerator for 1 hour. Add lemon juice in bag 5 minutes before grilling. Soak wooden skewers in water for 5 minutes and skewer marinated shrimp. Grill shrimp 3 to 4 minutes on each side. Shrimp should be opaque and firm. Sprinkle with chopped fresh basil before serving.

Stuffed Quinoa Bell Peppers

If you have been following along with my tips throughout this book, then you would know that the vitamin C in red bell peppers aids the absorption of iron in the beef. I always try to pair my beef with some form of fruit or vegetable that has vitamin C. If I can't, I'll squeeze a little lime juice on it.

⅓ cup quinoa, uncooked

½ tablespoon olive oil

½ tablespoon garlic, minced

½ pound lean ground beef

¼ teaspoon cumin

¼ teaspoon paprika

¼ teaspoon onion powder

¼ teaspoon chili powder

½ teaspoon salt

½ teaspoon black pepper

⅔ cup corn kernels

2 bell peppers

salsa (optional)

black beans, cooked (optional)

Instructions:

Preheat oven to 375°F. In a small saucepan, add 1 cup water and uncooked quinoa. Simmer on low heat, uncovered. Heat oil to medium-high heat in medium, nonstick pan and add garlic, ground beef, cumin, paprika, onion powder, chili powder, salt, and pepper. Cook and stir with a large spoon for 5 minutes or until meat is fully done. Mix in your cooked quinoa and corn kernels. Cut peppers in half and remove seeds and ribs. Place halved bell peppers in casserole or baking dish. Stuff peppers with cooked quinoa and beef filling. Add ⅓ cup water to bottom of dish. Bake for 18 to 20 minutes. Top with salsa and black beans, if desired.

Mexican Lasagna

Warning: Please wait for your Mexican Lasagna to cool before eating! I know it's tempting to dig in right away when you first pull it out of the oven and all that ooey-gooey cheese is in your face and the delicious aroma fills your kitchen, but I burned the roof of my mouth with a taste test. Don't be a hero, wait the 30 minutes. This also gives the lasagna time to reabsorb the juices that escaped from the turkey and tomatoes during the baking process.

2 tablespoons olive oil

1 lb. ground turkey

1 (15-oz.) can tomato sauce

½ teaspoon chili powder

½ teaspoon garlic powder

½ teaspoon onion powder

½ teaspoon paprika

1 teaspoon cumin

½ teaspoon salt

½ teaspoon black pepper

10 (6-inch) corn tortillas

1 (15-oz.) can fat-free refried beans

1 (8-oz.) can black olives, thinly sliced

2 plum tomatoes, diced

2 cups Mexican-blend shredded cheese

½ onion

Instructions:
Preheat oven to 375°F. In a large cooking pan, warm oil over medium heat and add ground turkey. Cook for 5 to 7 minutes or until fully cooked. Set aside to cool. Pour tomato sauce into a large bowl and add chili powder, garlic powder, onion powder, paprika, cumin, salt, and pepper. Mix with a whisk or spoon. Spread sauce across a large casserole dish. Lay down 2 to 3 tortillas on top of sauce. Next, scoop up a big spoonful of refried beans and spread atop tortillas. Again, scoop a large spoonful of cooked ground turkey and spread atop beans. Repeat this process with the olives, tomatoes, and lastly, cheese. Add more sauce on top of cheese and once again layer tortillas. Repeat entire process again. Add ¼ cup water to casserole dish, cover with foil. Bake for 35 minutes. Remove foil and bake for additional 10 minutes.

Teriyaki Mahi Mahi Pineapple Kabobs

I chose Mahi Mahi for this recipe because it's a firmer fish and will not fall apart on a grill. Salmon is also a good choice when grilling.

1 lb. Mahi Mahi, cut into 1½-inch cubes

1 lb. fresh pineapple, cut into 1½-inch cubes

2 green onion stems, cut into segments

½ cup low-sodium soy sauce

¼ cup rice vinegar

½ tablespoon coconut sugar

½ tablespoon honey

2 tablespoons sesame oil or coconut oil

½ teaspoon salt

½ teaspoon black pepper

1 tablespoon sesame seeds

Instructions:

Soak wooden skewers in water for 5 minutes. Skewer a piece of fish, pineapple, green onion, and repeat again until skewer is full. Be sure to leave 1 inch on the bottom and 1 inch on top of skewer. In a small bowl, mix remaining ingredients except sesame seeds for sauce. Brush sauce onto skewered fish, pineapple, and onion. Brush grill with coconut oil. Place skewers on grill. Cook for 8 to 12 minutes on medium-high heat and turn over every 2 to 3 minutes and baste with more sauce. Sprinkle with sesame seeds when done.

Buffalo Tofu Sticks

Tofu doesn't really have much flavor so it will taste like whatever you season it with. It's a good source of plant-based protein and used in many vegetarian dishes.

1 lb. extra-firm tofu, drained and pressed with paper towels

¾ cup Frank's Red Hot sauce

2½ cups panko crumbs

2 tablespoons milled flaxseed

½ teaspoon chili powder

½ teaspoon garlic powder

½ teaspoon onion powder

1 teaspoon salt

Instructions:
Preheat oven to 400°F. Slice tofu into 1-inch-thick sticks, place in large Ziploc bag with hot sauce, and marinate in refrigerator for 1 hour. In a large bowl, mix panko crumbs, flaxseed, chili powder, garlic powder, onion powder, and salt. Press marinated tofu into mixture and coat all sides evenly. Spray cookie sheet with oil and place tofu sticks on sheet. Bake for 15 minutes.

Tip: Flaxseed cannot be consumed whole; it needs to be ground to release its nutrients. If you don't have a mortar to grind your flaxseed, you can also use a coffee grinder, food processor, pepper grinder, or just buy it milled. Please remember to refrigerate once grinded; when the oils release, it can spoil. Each tablespoon of ground flaxseed contains 1.8 grams of plant omega-3s. My favorite ways to use flaxseed are in my smoothies and during baking.

Vegan Alfredo Sauce with Roasted Tomatoes and Mushrooms

I didn't tell my husband this sauce was vegan when he taste-tested it. He ate it, loved it, and asked for seconds. Then I proudly told him there was no cream or butter in it. Typical guy, he just shrugged his shoulders and said, "As long as it tastes good and I don't have to cook it, I don't care what's in it."

1 garlic bulb

2 shallots

1 cup cherry tomatoes

1½ cups crimini mushrooms

1 (14-oz.) can full-fat coconut cream

3 tablespoons olive oil

2 tablespoons salt

1 teaspoons black pepper

1 tablespoon cornstarch

Instructions:
Preheat oven 400°F. Cut top off garlic bulb and cut shallots in half. In a large bowl, add garlic, shallots, tomatoes, mushrooms, 2 tablespoons olive oil, 1 teaspoon salt, ½ teaspoon black pepper. Mix well and place on cookie sheet lined with parchment or wax paper. Bake for 15 minutes. Remove tomatoes and mushrooms and place in bowl for cooling. Place garlic and shallots back in oven for another 14 to 20 minutes. Allow cooling for 10 minutes. Squeeze out garlic cloves into blender; add shallots, coconut cream, remaining salt and pepper. Blend until smooth. Heat 1 tablespoon olive oil in a large pan and pour contents from blender into pan. Cook for 5 minutes on medium-low heat. In a small bowl, mix 2 tablespoons water and 1 tablespoon cornstarch until completely dissolved. Pour into sauce and stir while simmering for another 5 minutes on low heat.

Vegan Burger

When burgers come to mind, the last thing we think is *healthy*, but it can really happen. We just have to think outside the box and be open-minded—burgers don't always have to be ground beef. I got a little creative and used a mixture of lentils and crimini mushrooms to imitate the look and texture of ground beef. I also chose lentils because it's high in protein, which is important one thing to keep in mind when making vegetarian or vegan meals.

½ cup uncooked green lentils

2 tablespoons olive oil

2 cups crimini mushrooms, chopped

1½ tablespoons sunflower seeds

1 teaspoon garlic, minced

¼ onion, minced

½ teaspoon paprika

½ tablespoon Dijon mustard

1 tablespoon ketchup

1 teaspoon Worcestershire sauce

½ teaspoon salt

½ teaspoon black pepper

Instructions:

Place lentils in colander and rinse under water. In a small saucepan, add the lentils and 1¼ cup of water, bring up to a boil, down to a simmer, and cover with lid. Simmer for 15 to 20 minutes. Allow to cool for 10 minutes and blend in food processor to a chunky consistency.

Preheat a large, nonstick pan to medium, add ½ tablespoon olive oil and chopped crimini mushrooms. Cook for 5 minutes while occasionally stirring mushrooms around with a large cooking spoon. Drain any excess liquid.

In a large bowl, add lentils, mushrooms, sunflower seeds, garlic, onions, paprika, Dijon mustard, ketchup, Worcestershire sauce, salt, and pepper. Mix all ingredients by hand and mold into 4-ounce burger patties.

Heat a small nonstick pan on medium and add 1 teaspoon olive oil and 1 veggie burger patty. Cook 4 to 5 minutes on each side or until slightly crispy on the outside. Repeat cooking process with each veggie patty, but be sure to wipe pan with wet paper towel each time.

To serve, I recommend a thick bread like a Brioche bun, sliced in half, smeared with a little Dijon mustard, ketchup, sliced boiled beets, and topped with a big handful of microgreens.

Food Fact: If you want to keep this meal entirely vegan, make sure you choose a bread bun that has no dairy or eggs.

Creamy Butternut Squash Mac & Cheese

The key to great mac & cheese is the creamy sauce. The challenge for me was keeping the creamy texture, but cutting out most of the fat. I accomplished this by swapping out the butter, milk, and half the cheese with butternut squash. This recipe has only four ingredients. It's so easy; if you can boil water, you're already halfway done.

2 cups butternut squash, cubed

1½ cups light cheddar cheese, shredded

2 tablespoons Parmesan cheese, grated

8 oz. brown rice penne pasta, uncooked

Instructions:
Preheat oven to 375°F. In two large separate pots, bring water to boil. In first pot, add uncooked pasta, stirring occasionally for about 8 to 10 minutes. Remove from heat and drain pasta. In second pot, add butternut squash and also boil for 8 to 10 minutes. Drain most of water, leaving about ½ cup. In blender or food processor, blend butternut squash with the ½ cup of remaining boiled water until it reaches a smooth consistency. On a large cooking tray, mix in pasta, butternut squash, and cheddar cheese. Top with Parmesan cheese and bake for 15 minutes.

Tip: Women stop absorbing calcium around age twenty-five. Look at our bones as a savings account. For 25 to 30 years, you're saving calcium in your piggy bank, making mostly deposits and spending some daily on your body's needs. When your bank is full, you've reached your peak bone mass. You can no longer deposit calcium in your piggy bank, but you can make withdrawals. The more you take, the faster your bones deteriorate. Your body needs calcium to build and maintain strong bones. Too little calcium in your diet will lead you to take from your bank, thus causing osteoporosis. Adults 19 to 50 years old should consume 1000 milligrams of calcium a day.

Cheesy Turkey Meatballs

I grocery shop on the weekends and only buy enough to last a week. This means, come Friday, it's slim pickings. I made this with whatever I had in the refrigerator and freezer, which was ground turkey and zucchini. What's funny is the cheese stuffing is actually the girls' string cheese. What I find even more hilarious is that, instead of breadcrumbs, I toasted the heck out of the butt pieces of our sliced bread and crumbled that in. I always have to throw the end pieces out because the girls complain it's all crust! This is what happens when you grow up poor—you get very resourceful. The ingredients may not be fancy, but it sure looked and tasted good.

1 zucchini, chopped

1 slice whole grain bread

1 lb. lean ground turkey

1 egg

1 tablespoon garlic, minced

1 tablespoon dried oregano

½ teaspoon sea salt

½ teaspoon black pepper

2 pieces string cheese or 4 oz.
   mozzarella

2 tablespoons avocado oil

Instructions:
Preheat oven to 375°F. In food processor, blend zucchini until smooth and drain excess liquid. (I just used my blender.) Toast bread and crumble with your hands. In a large bowl, mix turkey, egg, zucchini, garlic, oregano, breadcrumbs, salt, and pepper. Cut cheese into 1-oz. sections. Roll mixture into meatballs twice the size of a golf ball and add cheese in center. Mold the meatball around the cheese with your hands. In oven-safe pan, warm oil over medium heat and cook each side of the meatballs 2 minutes. Bake for 20 minutes.

Marinara with Brown Rice Pasta

I envy my husband for falling asleep within a few minutes of closing his eyes. As I lay next to him, listening to his snoring, I think about my life and a lot of "what if"s. My most popular "what if" is: what I would do if the world came to an end and zombies took over? Well, you'll find me living at Costco because of the food and the equally important concrete walls. Then I start to think, what food would I miss most in the world and what I would stock pile? It wouldn't be cheeseburgers or pizza. For me, I would stock up on dried pasta and tomato sauce. I can eat spaghetti every day and not get tired of it.

1 small onion

2 tablespoons garlic, minced

2 tablespoons olive oil

5 roma tomatoes

1 (15-oz.) can plum tomatoes

2 tablespoons tomato paste

1 tablespoon oregano

large handful fresh basil

2 tablespoons coconut sugar

1½ tablespoons salt

½ tablespoon black pepper

1 (16-oz.) bag of brown rice spaghetti
   noodles

Instructions:
Blend onion, garlic, and olive oil until smooth in blender or food processor. Add to a large pot and cook on medium-low heat for 4 to 5 minutes. Blend remaining ingredients until smooth. (You can also do chunky.) Add to a large pot and mix everything. Cook until sauce starts to bubble and reduce heat to a simmer for another 15 to 20 minutes. Remove from heat and cool for 20 minutes. In a large pot, bring water to boil, add pasta, cook uncovered for 7 to 10 minutes, stirring occasionally to avoid clumping together. Drain pasta in colander. Scoop serving of pasta onto dinner plate and smother with sauce.

Broccoli Cheese Quesadilla

This recipe is simple, and it's one of those quick meals I make for the girls when I'm in a rush. We all enjoy it and Shayna just tolerates it, but at least she eats it! She prefers the version with cauliflower instead of broccoli, mainly because she can't see the cauliflower in the quesadilla.

2 cups broccoli florets, steamed

1½ cups cheddar cheese, shredded

½ tablespoon butter, melted

¼ cup milk

½ teaspoon onion powder

1 teaspoon salt

6 (8-inch) whole wheat or carb-balance flour tortillas

Instructions:

Blend broccoli, cheese, melted butter, milk, onion powder, and salt in food processor to a chunky texture. Spray a large, nonstick pan with oil, heat over medium low, add tortilla, scoop up filling, and add to half of tortilla. Fold other half of tortilla over filling. Cook for 2 to 3 minutes on each side until crispy. Repeat with remaining tortillas and filling.

Food Fact: It is a myth that gluten is unhealthy or bad for you. Gluten is a protein found in wheat endosperm. It's only unhealthy for people who are gluten-intolerant or have celiac disease. Yet, there are those who say that when they have cut out gluten from their diets, they've lost weight and felt better. The reason for this is simple: the foods gluten is added to are usually the unhealthy culprits. To cut out gluten, you would have to avoid all wheat-based flours and ingredients. Think about it: if gluten is added to a lot of foods, then the people who cut it out are eating more whole foods or "real food." That's why they lose weight and get healthier. Gluten itself is not the problem; everything served with it is.

Avocado on Toast

My go-to quick meal!

I wanted to share one of my favorite go-to meals when I don't have time to cook. I toast Naan bread with a little olive oil, sliced avocado, lime juice, chili flakes, and salt. It literally takes under ten minutes to make. I prefer Stonefire Naan bread, but toasted sliced bread works well, too.

Chickpea Greek Salad

If you're having trouble finding chickpeas in your grocery store they are also called garbanzo beans. Chickpeas will aid in weight loss because it's high in protein and fiber, therefore keeping you fuller longer.

For Salad

1 (14-oz.) can chickpeas

1 (6-oz.) can black olives

1½ cups cucumber, cubed

1½ cups grape tomatoes, halved

⅓ cup red onions, diced

1 cup feta cheese crumbles

½ teaspoon garlic powder

1 teaspoon salt

½ teaspoon black pepper

For Dressing

2 tablespoons olive oil

2 tablespoons balsamic vinegar

½ tablespoon lime juice

1 tablespoon honey

Instructions:

Drain and wash chickpeas and black olives. Slice olives in half. In a large bowl, add chickpeas, olives, cucumbers, tomatoes, red onions, feta cheese, garlic powder, salt, and pepper.

In a small bowl, whisk olive oil, balsamic vinegar, lime juice, and honey. Add dressing to salad and gently mix in with large spoon.

Steak Fajita Salad Bowl

Move over Chipotle, your salad bowls don't even compare to my steak fajita salad bowl. No longer will I settle for your skimpy steak portions or pay an extra $1.80 for guacamole. Homemade will always be better in price and taste.

For the steak:

12–14 ounces sirloin steak, thick cut (1½–2-inch thick cut)

½ teaspoon garlic powder

½ teaspoon onion powder

½ teaspoon salt

½ teaspoon black pepper

1 tablespoon avocado oil

For salad bowl:

½ cup uncooked quinoa

1 red bell pepper

1 green bell pepper

1 tablespoon avocado oil

1 tablespoon garlic, minced

1 teaspoon salt

1 avocado

juice of half a lime

2 heads romaine lettuce

2 mini Persian cucumbers or half English cucumber

1 cup grape tomatoes, halved

Instructions:

Season steak on both sides with garlic powder, onion powder, salt, and pepper. In a large, cast-iron pan, heat avocado to medium high. For medium steak, make sure pan is hot and sear steak on both sides for 3 to 4 minutes. Reduce to medium-low heat and cook for another 3 to 4 minutes on both sides.

Once the steak's ready, you can make the rest of the salad bowl. In small saucepan, pour 1 cup water and ½ cup uncooked quinoa. Bring to a boil and reduce to a simmer. Cook for 12 to 15 minutes or until liquid is absorbed and germ has spiraled out.

Slice red and green bell pepper and remove seeds and white membrane. In a large, nonstick pan, heat avocado oil to medium and add garlic, sliced bell peppers, and ½ teaspoon of salt. Cook for 3 to 4 minutes until al dente. Do not fully cook because peppers should still be crisp when eaten.

Thinly slice avocado and place in small bowl with lime juice and ½ teaspoon of salt. Chop romaine lettuce, wash in colander, and drain water. Slice steak.

Shrimp Scampi Tacos with Mango Avocado Salsa

My shrimp scampi with mango avocado salsa is one of the first recipes I shared on my blog. It's just as popular now as it was three years ago and I couldn't do my first cookbook without adding a fan favorite in the mix. The recipe came about by accident during a family get-a-way to Monterey. To save money on our vacation, I went to the grocery store by our condo and bought food to make instead of dining out. As soon as I walked in, I saw mango and avocado. I grabbed some of both and walked around the store waiting for inspiration for dinner. When I saw that shrimp was on sale, inspiration finally hit to make shrimp tacos with mango avocado salsa.

For Shrimp Scampi:

1 tablespoon olive oil

1 tablespoon garlic, minced

2 pounds shrimp, peeled and deveined

½ teaspoon salt

½ teaspoon black pepper

2 tablespoons parsley, chopped

juice of half a lime

For Mango Avocado Salsa:

1 mango, cubed

1 avocado, cubed

¼ cup cilantro, roughly chopped

¼ cup red onions, diced

juice of half a lime

½ teaspoon salt

½ teaspoon black pepper

Instructions:

In a nonstick pan, preheat olive oil to medium and add garlic. Cook until garlic is slightly brown, about 1 minute, and add shrimp, salt, and pepper. Cook shrimp 2 minutes on each side. Add parsley and lime juice and cook for another minute.

In a large bowl, mix mango, avocado, cilantro, red onions, lime juice, salt, and pepper.

I used yellow corn tortillas for my tacos. Add 3 to 4 pieces of shrimp scampi on top of your taco and top with scoop of mango avocado salsa.

MEAL PREPPING WITH SLOW COOKER DINNERS

This chapter will be life-changing, I promise. The number one reason I hear people use for not cooking at home is that they don't have enough time. Well, I'm changing the game for you busy bees. Imagine, after a long day of work, you open the door to your house and are greeted with the rich aroma of dinner, already prepared for you. You kick off those high heels, unhook that bra, put on a t-shirt, and take a seat on the couch, ready to relax and surf Netflix. It's not a dream; it can really happen.

I took a chapter from my Pro Fitness Athlete buddies on meal prepping and, of course, added my twist to it. If you're unfamiliar, just know that when they're training for competitions, they make their meals in advance. All of the meals are portioned out and weighed. The purpose is to make sure they meet the correct macronutrients to result in the physique. I'm using this same concept, but to save time. How amazing would it be to come home from a long day of work and already have dinner ready?

The solution is so simple, I'm surprised more are not doing it already. Slow cooker dinners are already a huge time-saver because you just set it and forget it, but I took it one step further: meal prepping your dinners and storing them in freezer bags. This way you can wake up, throw your previously frozen and prepped meal in your slow cooker, and have dinner ready when you get home. When meal prepping, don't just make one bag; make as many as you like. The time it takes to prepare five is only slightly more than making one. It's one grocery shopping trip, one time washing and cutting vegetables, one time cutting meat, one time cleaning up. Yet you can yield 1 to 5 meals depending how committed you are. Spare a few hours of your lazy Sunday and then kick back your feet when you walk in the door on Monday (and Tuesday, and Wednesday . . .). Or save it in the freezer for when your week gets hectic and you have no time to cook. When prepping slow cooker dinners, you get the convenience of frozen dinners, but also a home-cooked, nutritious meal.

Slow Cooker Chicken Sausage
   Jambalaya   131
Slow Cooker Vegan Chili   132
Beef Stew   135

Coconut Chicken Curry   137
Turkey Sloppy Joes   138
Balsamic Pulled Chicken   141
Chicken Tortilla Soup   142

Slow Cooker Chicken Sausage Jambalaya

The perfect addition to this meal would be shrimp, but adding it to a slow cooker for 6 hours would overcook it. I didn't add it to the original recipe because the purpose was to set it and forget it. If you have the time, you can add 1 pound of peeled shrimp into the slow cooker the last 30 minutes of cooking.

4–6 chicken sausage links (My favorite is Aidell's chicken apple sausage)

1½ cups brown rice, uncooked

1 cup celery, chopped

½ cup onion, chopped

½ cup green bell peppers, chopped

1 can tomatoes, diced

1 tablespoon garlic, minced

¼ cup Worcestershire sauce

1½ tablespoons paprika

2 bay leaves

½ tablespoon dried oregano

½ tablespoon dried thyme

½ tablespoon onion powder

½ tablespoon salt

½ tablespoon black pepper

Instructions:

Defrost freezer bag overnight in refrigerator or soak in warm water for 1 hour before adding to slow cooker. Add 3 cups water or chicken stock and cook on low for 5 to 6 hours.

Microwaving your kitchen sponge for two minutes can kill most bacteria. Our kitchen sponge comes into contact with the food we prepare in the kitchen. The cutting board used to cut raw chicken is scrubbed with a sponge and soap, but the same sponge is used to wash other dishes. Replace your sponges often and microwave them in between.

Slow Cooker Vegan Chili

Black beans, pinto beans, and lentils are a good source of protein. Try this recipe for your next Meatless Monday.

1 (15-oz.) can black beans

1 (15-oz.) can pinto beans

1 (15-oz.) can diced tomatoes

½ cup uncooked lentils

1 small red pepper, diced

1 small green pepper, diced

1 cup carrots, chopped

½ onion, diced

1 cup celery, chopped

1 tablespoon minced garlic

1½ tablespoons ground cumin

½ tablespoon onion powder

1 tablespoon tomato paste

2 bay leaves

1 teaspoon oregano

½ tablespoon salt

½ tablespoon black pepper

½ tablespoon chili powder

Instructions:
Defrost freezer bag overnight in refrigerator or soak in warm water for 1 hour before adding to slow cooker. Add 3 cups water or vegetable stock and cook on low for at least 5 to 6 hours.

Beef Stew

The first time I made this, it was too watery because I forgot the flour and didn't add enough potatoes. You really need the flour and the starch from the potatoes to thicken the stew. The thick consistency is perfect for dipping a big piece of crusty bread in.

1½–2 lb. beef chuck

¼ cup whole wheat flour

3 carrots, sliced

1 celery stalk, chopped

3 red potatoes, cubed

½ onion, diced

⅓ cup red wine

1 tablespoon Worcestershire sauce

2 tablespoons olive oil

1 tablespoon minced garlic

1 bay leave

1 teaspoon thyme

½ teaspoon paprika

½ teaspoon salt

½ teaspoon black pepper

1½ cups beef broth

Instructions:

In a large freezer bag, add beef and flour. Seal bag and shake up until flour coats all of the beef. Add the remaining ingredients except broth. Freeze until ready to cook. Defrost bag in a large bowl overnight in refrigerator. Pour defrosted contents into slow cooker; add broth and cook on medium for at least 8 hours.

Take steak out of the refrigerator 20 minutes before cooking to bring to room temperature. Cold steaks will cook unevenly, overcooked on the outside and undercooked on the inside. After cooking, let steaks rest for at least 10 minutes. Cutting into your steak too soon will release all the juices and leave it dry.

Coconut Chicken Curry

It should be no surprise that I love Asian food since I'm Vietnamese. And it shouldn't be a surprise that the coconut chicken curry recipe is my favorite slow cooker recipe. It just reminds me of meals my parents made for me when I was still living at home.

8–10 chicken thighs

1½ cups wild rice

6 green onion stems, chopped

1 small onion, chopped

1 (15-oz.) can light coconut milk

2 tablespoons curry powder

1 tablespoon turmeric powder

2 tablespoons fish sauce or soy sauce

2 tablespoons apple cider vinegar

2 tablespoons coconut sugar

1 tablespoon garlic, minced

1 tablespoon ginger, grated

1 bay leaf

2 tablespoons olive oil

½ tablespoon salt

½ tablespoon black pepper

Instructions:
Defrost freezer bag overnight in refrigerator or soak in warm water for 1 hour before adding to slow cooker. Add 2½ cups water, coconut water, or chicken stock and cook on high for 4 to 5 hours.

Turkey Sloppy Joes

Growing up, the only time I had sloppy joes was from my middle school cafeteria. I loved eating them, but it was so messy that I didn't have it often for fear of embarrassing myself at school. Now as an adult, I pretty much don't care about being cool anymore so bring on the wet naps!

For Sloppy Joes:

1½–2 lb. lean ground turkey

1 cup carrots, chopped

1 (15-oz.) can tomatoes

1 small red bell pepper, diced

½ medium onion, diced

⅓ cup ketchup

¼ cup Worcestershire sauce

2 tablespoons Dijon mustard

2 tablespoons apple cider vinegar

1 tablespoon garlic, minced

½ tablespoon onion powder

½ garlic powder

½ tablespoon salt

½ tablespoon black pepper

For sandwich:

6-8 brioche buns

1 cup cheddar cheese, shredded

Instructions:

Defrost freezer bag overnight in refrigerator or soak in warm water for 1 hour before adding to crock pot. Add 1½ cups water or chicken stock and cook on high for 4 to 5 hours. I suggest using a sandwich bread that is really thick, like a brioche bun, that way your bread can absorb the sauce without falling apart. Slice brioche bun in half, scoop up some sloppy joe onto half of bun, sprinkle some cheddar cheese, and top with other half of bun.

Balsamic Pulled Chicken

My balsamic pulled chicken is my healthier version of pulled pork.

Chicken:

2–3 chicken breast fillets

2 cups coconut water

1 cup water or chicken stock

⅓ cup apple cider vinegar

1 onion

1 bay leaf

1 tablespoon garlic

2 tablespoons olive oil

½ tablespoon salt

½ tablespoon black pepper

Balsamic Sauce:

⅓ cup balsamic vinegar

¼ cup oyster sauce

⅓ cup ketchup

1 tablespoon garlic, minced

1 tablespoon coconut sugar

1 teaspoon salt

Instructions:

Add all ingredients to slow cooker and cook on low for 6 to 7 hours. Remove chicken and shred with two forks. Remove bay leaf and add shredded chicken back into slow cooker.

For Balsamic Sauce, add all ingredients into small bowl and whisk together.

In a nonstick pan, add 1 teaspoon of olive oil and 2 tablespoon of balsamic sauce. Heat on low until sauce starts to bubble and thicken. Scoop (4 to 5 oz.) of shredded chicken, let most of the broth drip off before adding chicken to saucepan. Simmer until sauce is thick, about 3 to 4 minutes, and has absorbed into chicken. Add to whole wheat burger bun or bread of your choice.

Optional: Add ⅓ cup of my homemade broccoli slaw (page 71).

Chicken Tortilla Soup

You can choose not to use canned beans and make this your own if you're worried about the extra sodium added. For me, the choice to save time outweighs the extra sodium. I buy low-sodium canned beans, dump it all in a colander, and rinse off all the juice and only use the beans.

4 chicken breast fillets

1 strip nitrate-free, center-cut bacon

1 can black beans

1½ cups chicken stock

1 cup coconut water

1 (15-oz.) can tomato sauce

2 cloves garlic, minced

1 green bell pepper, diced

½ onion, diced

½ tablespoon cumin

1 teaspoon chili powder

½ tablespoon sea salt

½ tablespoon black pepper

1 bag blue corn tortilla chips

Instructions:
Place all ingredients in slow cooker and cook 4 to 5 hours on high. Take chicken breast out and shred with 2 forks and add back to crockpot. Serve with blue corn tortilla chips.

SMOOTHIES, SHAKES & DESSERTS

I can't believe I'm in my thirties and have only now discovered how much I love smoothies and shakes. Before, I looked at them as diet drinks and would religiously drink a Slimfast chocolate shake every morning for breakfast. It was totally disgusting and had twenty-plus ingredients I can't even identify, but I drank it anyway because I thought it would make me skinny. I don't know what I was thinking back then—maybe it was my tight jeans cutting oxygen to my brain. Whatever the reason, I'm glad that I eat and drink with purpose now. Now, if I really want a chocolate shake in the morning, I'll blend almond milk, banana, yogurt, vanilla extract, and cacao nibs. I add those ingredients because I want calcium for strong bones, potassium for lower blood pressure, and antioxidants for a stronger immune system. Even though I am more mindful of what I eat, it doesn't mean I sacrifice taste, though.

Don't think you can't indulge in dessert either! In my book, you can have your cake and eat it, too. You can make almost any dessert healthier by simply swapping out a few ingredients. You just have to be a little creative, opened minded, and inventive. Or you can just use the recipes I already developed in this lovely cookbook!

Green Tea Green Smoothie   144
Mint Chocolate Chip Smoothie   145
Chocolate Peanut Butter Protein
    Shake   145
Basil Strawberry & Watermelon
    Smoothie   146
Vanilla Coffee Shake   146
Pear Berry Green Smoothie   149
Piña Colada Smoothie   149
Kali-Fornia Smoothie   150
Orange Coconut Cream Smoothie   150
Creamy Avocado Shake   151
Cinnamon Apple Green Smoothie   153

Shayna & Kiera's Strawberry Banana
    Smoothie   154
Almond Joy Bites   154
Chunky Monkey Frozen Yogurt   157
Mango Black Sticky Rice   159
Baked Blueberry Quinoa Donuts   160
Granola Bars   163
Flourless Peanut Butter & Jelly Cookies   165
Strawberry Fruit Leathers   167
Watermelon Jell-O   169
Cinnamon Oatmeal Stuffed Apple   171

Green Tea Green Smoothie

Smoothies are my version of fast food. I especially love green smoothies because they're so nutrient dense. My good friend, Jadah Sellner, was the first person to introduce green smoothies to me. When she explained to me that she blended spinach and fruit together for breakfast, I was skeptical it would taste good. (I think I turned a little green with just the idea of drinking spinach.) It wasn't until New Year's morning 2012, after a sleepover at the Sellners, that she finally convinced me to try one. Well, actually if you want to get technical, it wasn't until I saw my twins drinking and enjoying them that I finally took a tentative sip.

That first taste changed my life forever. I loved it and can honestly say I have a green smoothie three or four days a week. Do not fear the green color, folks. If you have the proper ratio of greens to fruit, it will taste sweet. If my three-year-old twins can drink them, so can you. You can knock out a good chunk of your daily fruit and veggie recommendation in just one drink. Not only are they nutrient-dense, but they're also low in calories, high in fiber, and take less than 5 minutes to make. They also never get boring because you can do so many combinations of fruit and veggies. One smoothie can be a full meal in a glass. Make sure you have a high-quality blender so your smoothies are not chunky.

1 cup brewed green tea (cold)

2 cups spinach

⅓ cup parsley

2 oz. cucumber

1 pear

½ banana

¾ cup ice

Instructions:
Add all ingredients into blender and blend.

Mint Chocolate Chip Smoothie

Cacao nibs are rich in antioxidants, but taste quite bitter. Whenever adding something bitter like cacao nibs to your smoothies, make sure you balance it with something sweet like honey, dates, or a very ripe banana.

2 cups spinach

⅓ cup mint

1 tablespoon cacao nibs

½ banana

1 tablespoon honey

1 cup coconut milk

½ cup ice

Instructions:
Add all indigents into blender and blend until smooth.

Chocolate Peanut Butter Protein Shake

This is my go-to pre-workout shake. It's the perfect balance of protein, healthy fats, and carbohydrates. It gives me plenty of fuel during my exercise without feeling too full. For protein, I use Greek yogurt instead of protein powders. One cup of non-fat Greek yogurt is only 130 calories, but packs a whopping 23 grams of protein. That's the same amount of protein in three eggs!

½ tablespoon 100% cacao powder

⅓ cup peanut butter powder or

   1 tablespoon peanut butter

½ cup plain non-fat Greek yogurt

½ banana

½ tablespoon milled flaxseed

1 cup almond milk

1 oz. semi-sweet dark chocolate

¾ cup ice

Instructions:
Add all ingredients into blender and blend until smooth.

Basil Strawberry & Watermelon Smoothie

Not gonna lie—this is a virgin version of an adult beverage I serve at parties. I just took out the vodka, but kept the fancy martini glass. You can also spear strawberries with toothpicks instead of olives to class it up a bit.

6–7 strawberries

1 cup watermelon

5–6 basil leaves

1 teaspoon lime juice

¼ teaspoon salt

¾ cup ice

Instructions:
Add all ingredients into blender and blend until smooth.

Vanilla Coffee Shake

Hit two birds with one stone by having your coffee and breakfast together. This is perfect for those really early mornings when you need that jolt of caffeine, but it's a bit too early for a full breakfast.

1 cup black coffee

1 teaspoon vanilla extract

1 cup plain Greek yogurt

⅓ cup almond milk

1 tablespoon honey

¾ cup ice

Instructions:
Add all ingredients into blender and blend until smooth.

Pear Berry Green Smoothie

Try this smoothie if you're not meeting your daily requirements for fiber. Pears, strawberries, and chia seeds are all high in fiber.

2 cups spinach

⅓ cup parsley

1 pear

6–7 strawberries

1 cup coconut water

½ tablespoon chia seeds

¾ cup ice

Instructions:
Blend everything except chia seeds. Wait to top drink after blending or most of the chia seeds will stick to the inside of the blender.

Piña Colada Smoothie

Cutting pineapple just to make a smoothie is too much work. For fruit like pineapple and mangoes, buy them pre-cut and frozen already. Saves you a lot of time.

2 cups Swiss chard

2 cups pineapple

1 cup coconut water

½ cup coconut cream

1 tablespoon honey

⅔ cup ice

Instructions:
Add all ingredients into blender and blend until smooth.

Kali-Fornia Smoothie

Kale is rougher in texture than other leafy greens and needs special treatment when using it for smoothies. If you don't have a good quality blender, I suggest first blending your kale with your liquid and then blending the remaining ingredients.

2 cups kale (remove stems)

⅓ avocado

1 banana

5–6 strawberries

1 cup coconut water

1 teaspoon chia seeds

¾ cup ice

Instructions:
Blend kale and coconut water first until smooth. Add everything except chia seeds and blend again. Sprinkle your smoothie with chia seeds after blending. Most chia seeds will get stuck on the inner sides of the blender if you try to blend them.

Orange Coconut Cream Smoothie

Another option with my orange coconut cream smoothie recipe is to make popsicles, minus the ice. If you don't have popsicle molds, ice cube trays with toothpicks work just fine, too! Use the silicon molds so it's easy to pop them out.

1 orange, peeled

1 teaspoon orange peel zest

½ cup coconut cream

¾ cup coconut water

4–5 pitted dates

¾ cup ice

Instructions:
Add all ingredients to blender and blend. Unless you have a high-quality blender, pitted dates don't blend that great. My trick is to soak 4 to 5 dates in 1 cup water overnight to rehydrate them before blending.

Creamy Avocado Shake

This avocado shake is so thick and creamy, I actually like eating it with a spoon instead of drinking it. It's a great, sweet snack in the middle of the day and we love making popsicles with it as well.

For shake:

½ avocado

1 banana

½ tablespoon honey

1 cup almond milk

Instructions:
Blend all ingredients until smooth.

For popsicles:

1 avocado

1 ripe banana

2 tablespoons honey

1½ cups almond milk

Instructions:
Blend all ingredients until smooth, pour into popsicle molds, and freeze for at least 2½ hours.

Tip: To get the kids involved, use ice cube trays instead of popsicle molds and stick toothpicks in them.

Cinnamon Apple Green Smoothie

When I drink a green smoothie in the morning, I feel like I set the precedent for the rest of the day. It actually encourages me to continue making healthy choices throughout the day. For me, the darker the green smoothie the better—it makes me feel like I'm drinking in a lot of nutrients and vitamins.

2 cups kale

1 apple

3–4 dates, pitted

½ teaspoon cinnamon

1 cup water

½ cup ice

Instructions:
Add all ingredients into blender and blend until smooth.

Tip: Frozen fruits and vegetables can be healthier than fresh from the grocery store. As soon as a fruit or vegetable is picked, it starts to lose nutrients. Frozen fruits and vegetables are picked when they are ripe and frozen to lock in nutrients. A lot of produce at the supermarkets is picked before it's ripe, artificially ripened during transport, and then travels hundreds of miles before being sold. Freezing naturally preserves food; therefore, no additives are needed. It's also a time-saver: the fruits and vegetables are already cut up and prepared for you.

Shayna & Kiera's Strawberry Banana Smoothie

I make this a lot for the twins because we always have the large bag of frozen strawberries from Costco and bananas as a base that I use often for my smoothies. I recommend this smoothie for nutritious snack in between lunch and dinner. Just because I make it for the twins doesn't mean adults can't enjoy it as well. Harlen often makes this same recipe with a scoop of protein after his workouts.

1 banana
8–12 frozen strawberries
1 tablespoon honey
1 tablespoon milled flaxseed
1½ cups almond milk

Instructions:
Add all ingredients into blender and blend until smooth.

Almond Joy Bites

Candy is my weakness. I cannot have any candy in the house or else I'll be hiding wrappers beneath the sofa cushions. This was my way of satisfying my sweet tooth and also controlling how much sugar is in each bite.

2 cups unsweetened coconut, shredded
¾ cup maple syrup
¼ cup coconut oil

½ cup raw almonds
2 cups dark chocolate chunks
1 tablespoon coarse salt

Instructions:
Blend coconut, maple syrup, and coconut oil in food processor or blender. Spray ice cube molds with coconut oil and fill with coconut mixture. Place in freezer for 30 minutes. Remove frozen coconut molds with butter knife. Gently press an individual almond on each coconut mold. Add chocolate to small glass bowl and microwave for 90 seconds. (If you don't have dark chocolate chunks or chips, use a dark chocolate bar and roughly chop it with a large knife.) Remove from microwave and stir until the rest of the chocolate melts. Place wax paper below cookie rack to collect dripped chocolate. Pick up each piece and dip the bottom into the chocolate and place on rack. Spoon remaining chocolate on top and spread with your spoon to cover the sides. Sprinkle with coarse salt and place back in freezer for 30 minutes.

Chunky Monkey Frozen Yogurt

The first time I had Ben & Jerry's Chunky Monkey ice cream was in college. In fact, I blame Ben & Jerry for some of my freshman weight gain. I've learned moderation since then, but I can indulge all I want in my healthier version. Harlen swears it tastes just like banana cheesecake, but I'll let you decide for yourself.

2 bananas

½ cup plain yogurt, bonus protein points if you choose Greek yogurt

1 cup dark chocolate chips

4 waffle cones

½ cup coconut cream

1 tablespoon honey

pinch of salt

handful of walnuts

Instructions:

Slice bananas and freeze in Ziploc bag. Slicing bananas makes them easier to blend. Freeze yogurt in ice cube trays. Melt chocolate in a small bowl for 1 minute in microwave. You can also use a double boiler if you want to do it the long way (and like doing dishes). Stir until smooth and scoop melted chocolate into cone, flip cone upside down, and rotate cone until chocolate coats the entire inside. I like this method because it protects the cone from getting soggy. Put cones on wax paper and place in refrigerator for 15 minutes. Once your banana and yogurt are frozen, add them to your blender with the coconut cream, honey, and salt. Blend until smooth. There is not a lot of liquid so you might have to stop your blender 1 or 2 times to push contents down from the sides to blend well. Top with walnuts.

Did you know *that in the United States 30 to 40 percent of the food supply is wasted? That's more than 20 pounds of food per person a month. Thirty percent of the food we grow is never eaten. It all starts with us, the consumer. It's not just about not finishing the food on your plate or the veggies in the fridge going bad; it's a bigger global problem. We, as consumers, do not want to purchase imperfect food, like a misshapen apple or a crooked carrot. Grocery stores know this and do not purchase them for their shelves, and farmers are aware of this and discard foods that do not look perfect. Most of the food waste is not what we toss out from our refrigerator, but occurs at the start of production, harvesting, and processing. How do we stop food waste? To me, it really falls in the hands of the consumer.*

Mango Black Sticky Rice

The story behind black rice, or "Forbidden Rice," is that back when China was ruled by an emperor, the rice was only cultivated for his consumption. Even though it's now available for everyone, it's still more expensive than white or brown rice. I was able to find it at a bulk food bin section at my local grocery store, which is a lot less than buying it packaged. Black rice has similar nutrition benefits to brown rice with higher amounts of antioxidants, protein and double the fiber. It has sticky texture and a nutty taste. I'm guessing black rice will one day be just as popular as kale.

½ cup uncooked black rice

½ cup maple syrup

1 tablespoon cornstarch

1 can light coconut milk (400mL)

1 tablespoon stevia

2 mangos

¼ cup shredded, unsweetened coconut

Instructions:
In small saucepan add 2 cups water and black rice, bring to a boil, then reduce to a simmer. Simmer for 30 to 40 minutes uncovered, stirring occasionally. Cool for 10 minutes and stir in maple syrup. In small saucepan add coconut milk and stevia, then simmer for 2 to 3 minutes. Mix cornstarch in ¼ cup water until diluted and stir into coconut milk. Simmer for another 2 minutes while stirring. Cool for 15 minutes and sauce will thicken. To serve, slice mango on a plate, add black rice, pour coconut sauce, and sprinkle with shredded coconut.

Baked Blueberry Quinoa Donuts

I'm a cheater; I use store-bought cake frosting for my glaze. Before you take away my mommy card, let me explain. I tried making a "healthier" frosting with coconut cream, coconut sugar, and coconut oil. Not gonna lie—it tasted all kinds of weird. I also researched a few more alternatives like dusting the donuts in just coconut sugar, but in the end, I went with what I knew my kids would like. Don't be too hard on yourself and look at the facts. The ingredients are healthy, it's baked and not fried, and a light drizzle of frosting will have your kids gobbling up these donuts.

1½ cups oats

1 cup wheat flour

1 cup almond milk

1 egg

½ tablespoon chia seeds

1 tablespoon coconut sugar

½ tablespoon baking soda

1 teaspoon sea salt

½ cup blueberries

Instructions:
Preheat oven to 350°F. Blend oats in your blender or food processor until they reach a fine consistency. In a large bowl, mix in all ingredients except for blueberries. In a nonstick six-donut pan, pour mixture into each donut mold, filling it only halfway. Drop a few blueberries in each donut mold. Bake for 10 minutes or until golden brown. I heated ½ cup of store-bought frosting in the microwave for 15 seconds, poured it in a Ziploc bag, cut a small piece of the corner off, and "lightly" drizzled the melted frosting over the donuts.

Tip: For remaining batter, pour in freezer bag and freeze. Saves you a lot of time and means fewer dishes to wash next time you make it.

Granola Bars

This recipe came about when I was cleaning out my pantry. I had all these random ingredients sitting around and threw them together to make granola bars. Don't feel like you need to stick to this recipe exactly. Have fun with it and add your favorite dried fruits, nuts, and seeds.

3 cups raisin granola (you can also use
    regular granola or oats)

1 tablespoon flaxseed, milled

¼ cup goji berries

2 cups dark chocolate morsels

½ tablespoon cinnamon

2 tablespoons butter or coconut oil,
    melted

⅓ cup honey

½ tablespoon vanilla extract

Instructions:

Preheat oven to 350°F. In a large bowl, add granola, milled flaxseed, goji berries, ¼ cup dark chocolate, cinnamon melted butter, honey, and vanilla extract. Mix with spatula until ingredients are evenly distributed. Line a medium-sized baking dish with wax paper. Pour granola mixture on top of wax paper or spray cooking pan with oil. Press granola mix down with spatula, making sure to pack ingredients in tight. Bake for 15 minutes. Remove from oven and cool for 15 minutes. Microwave the remaining chocolate in a small bowl for 1 to 1½ minutes and stir with spatula until all chocolate is melted. Spread melted chocolate on top of granola, covering the entire surface. Place another sheet of wax paper on top. Place in freezer for 1 hour. Peel wax paper off top and cut into squares.

Flourless Peanut Butter & Jelly Cookies

Peanut flour is my new obsession! This is an all-natural flour made by grinding peanuts and removing most of the oil, which means removing most of the fat. It's really not flour, but made into that consistency. If you followed my tips section about bulk bins, that's where you will mostly likely find peanut flour. It has less fat than regular peanut butter because the oil is removed, but still tastes like the original. Peanut flour is also a great addition to your smoothies if you're looking to add more protein.

Strawberry Jelly:

1 cup frozen strawberries

2 tablespoons honey

1 tablespoon coconut sugar

1 teaspoon lemon juice

1 packet gelatin

¼ cup water

Cookies:

2 cups peanut butter flour

½ cup honey

1 tablespoon coconut sugar

1 egg

½ cup avocado oil

½ teaspoon baking powder

½ teaspoon salt

For the Jelly:
Mix all ingredients in small saucepan. Bring to a boil and then simmer. Simmer for 10 minutes, stirring occasionally. Pour contents into blender and blend until fine. Pour sauce into jar and refrigerate for at least 1 hour to cool and thicken.

For the Cookies:
Preheat oven to 350°F. Mix all ingredients by hand and roll into 2-oz. balls. Gently press thumb into dough to make a crater for your jelly. Line cookie sheet with wax paper and place cookies on top. Bake for 15 minutes. Cool for 5 minutes and add a dollop of your strawberry jelly into crater.

Strawberry Fruit Leathers

Remember the strawberry jelly we made for the peanut butter cookies (page 165)? Well, I doubled up on the recipe and made my version of fruit roll-ups, minus the coconut sugar and gelatin.

2 cups frozen strawberries

4 tablespoon honey

2 teaspoon lemon juice

½ cup water

Instructions:

Preheat oven to 170°F. Mix all ingredients in small saucepan. Bring to a boil and then reduce to a simmer. Simmer for 10 to 15 minutes, stirring occasionally. Pour contents into blender and blend until smooth. Pour sauce into jar and refrigerate for at least 1 hour to cool and thicken. Line a rimmed baking sheet with a silicone baking mat or foil. Pour contents from blender onto cookie sheet and spread evenly with spatula. Bake for 3 to 4 hours. Cool. Place parchment paper on top and press over gently. Grab corner of parchment paper and slowly peel fruit leather off cookie sheet.

Food Fact: Honey is the only food that does not expire. Honey is low in moisture and low PH levels create an environment that bacteria cannot survive in. The oldest honey found was 5,000 years old in Georgia. Would you try it?

Watermelon Jell-O

Back when I partied like a rock star (a.k.a. before kids), my best friend, Vicky, would make the best Jell-O shots for her annual White Elephant party. Every year, she would up her game to different flavors, colors, and percentage of alcohol. She out-did herself one year using oranges instead of the regular, old, boring plastic shot cups. She cut them in half, scooped out the fruit, and replaced it with vodka Jell-O. We sliced them up, sprayed whipped cream on them, and by the end of the night, my husband had to be carried to the car. That's pretty much where I got the concept for this recipe—minus the hangover.

1 mini watermelon

½ cup water

4 (.25-oz.) packets of gelatin

Instructions:
Cut watermelon in half, scoop out fruit, and add to juicer. You can also blend and strain. Use rubber spatula to push and press pulp against the strainer to get most of the juice into a large bowl. You only want the juice, not the pulp. In a small saucepan, boil water and ½ cup of the watermelon juice. Remove from heat and mix in gelatin powder. Mix and stir so gelatin doesn't clump and then pour back into bowl mixing again.
Place your watermelon halves in small bowls so they stay upright. Pour juice back into watermelon halves and refrigerate for at least 2 hours or until firm.

Food Fact: *Foods high in fiber control weight loss and clean the intestines. Most people do not have enough fiber in their diets. Fiber has two roles in my book; it slows down glucose absorption and takes longer to digest, therefore helping you feel fuller longer and helping in weight loss. Fiber also aids in cleaning out the digestive tract. The roughage from fiber helps food move through your digestive tract and absorbs water to help eliminate waste and toxins from your body. It is recommended that adults consume about 25 to 35 grams of fiber a day, but the average American takes in only about 15 grams a day. If you're not used to a high-fiber diet, ease in slowly by adding a little more every day.*

Cinnamon Oatmeal Stuffed Apple

I swear this tastes so much like apple pie, I've been tempted to add a big scoop of vanilla ice cream to it. The smell from the oven reminds me of fall.

1 cup rolled oats, uncooked

1 teaspoon cinnamon

1 teaspoon nutmeg

4 large red apples

1 tablespoon coconut sugar

shaved dark chocolate (optional)

Instructions:
Boil 2 cups of water. In a large bowl, pour boiled water, oats, cinnamon, nutmeg, and coconut sugar. Let soak for 5 minutes.

Preheat oven to 375°F. Slice tops off apples and cut/scoop out inside. Stuff cooked oats into apples. Place apples on cooking pan and add a quarter inch of water to bottom of pan. Bake for 20 minutes. Add shaved dark chocolate—optional for some, but for us it's a must.

ACKNOWLEDGMENTS

I would like to thank my family, friends, and colleagues for their support, encouragement, and love: my mom, Thu Van Tran, who is the backbone of our family, and who I want to be when I grow up; my dad, Ngan Nguyen, for wanting a better life for us and having the courage to leave everything behind to bring us to the United States; my older brother, Le Nguyen, who is proof positive that you can accomplish anything if you set your mind to it; my little brother, Kiem Nguyen, who puts his blood, sweat, and tears in the pursuit of his passion and dreams; my little sister, Nga Nguyen, who acts more like the older sister by always looking out for me; my sister-in-law Christy Nguyen, who talks to me for hours every day about nothing and everything; my sister-in-law, Catherine Ramos, who inspires and motivates me to be more organized in work and life; my mother-in-law, Norma Morales, for her unselfish commitment to her grandchildren and taking care of them when I need to focus on work; my father-in-law, Harlen Morales Sr., who can fix anything and everything we ask no matter how busy he is; my friend, Jadah Sellner, who mentored me and gave me my first green smoothie; Vicky Tran-Vasquez, my best friend, sometimes therapist, and cheerleader; my makeup artist, Elaine Sanusi, for making me beautiful inside and out; my managers, Lily Berg and Alexandria, for taking my career to the next level and making sure the mortgage gets paid; and my literary agent, Laura Yorke, for her guidance and commitment throughout this book-creating process.

I'd also like to thank my editor, Nicole Frail, and the team at Skyhorse Publishing for working so hard to bring this book to life.

INDEX

A

Almond Butter, 33
Almond Joy Bites, 154
Apples
    Baked Cinnamon Apple French Toast Casserole, 35
    Cinnamon Apple Green Smoothie, 153
    Cinnamon Oatmeal Stuffed Apple, 171
    Shredded Broccoli Slaw, 71
Applesauce
    Banana Bread Muffins, 42
Asian Collard Green Wraps, 81
Asparagus
    Baked Lemon Asparagus, 83
    Tofu Veggie Stir Fry, 99
Avocado
    Baked Avocado & Eggs, 45
    Baked Vegetarian Taco Bowls, 86
    Creamy Avocado Shake, 151
    Fully Loaded Baked Yams, 53
    Guacamole, 63
    Salmon Avocado Ceviche, 79
    Shrimp Scampi Tacos with Mango Avocado
        Salsa, 127
    storage of, 45
Avocado oil, 21
Avocado on Toast, 121

B

Bacon
    BLT Summer Rolls, 57
    Chicken Tortilla Soup, 142
Baked Avocado & Eggs, 45
Baked Blueberry Quinoa Donuts, 160
Baked Cinnamon Apple French Toast Casserole, 35
Baked Lemon Asparagus, 83
Baked Vegetarian Taco Bowls, 86

Balsamic Pulled Chicken, 141
Banana
    Creamy Avocado Shake, 151
    Green Tea Green Smoothie, 144
    Mint Chocolate Chip Smoothie, 145
    Shayna & Kiera's Strawberry Banana Smoothie, 154
Banana Bread Muffins, 42
Basil
    Basil Strawberry & Watermelon Smoothie, 146
    Kale Basil Pesto, 102
    Mini Eggplant Pizza, 78
    Roasted Caprese Kabobs, 51
    Sundried Tomato & Basil Frittata, 41
Basil Strawberry & Watermelon Smoothie, 146
Beans
    black
        Chicken Tortilla Soup, 142
        Fully Loaded Baked Yams, 53
        Slow Cooker Vegan Chili, 132
        Stuffed Quinoa Bell Peppers, 107
    cannellini, 76
    pinto
        Slow Cooker Vegan Chili, 132
    refried
        Mexican Lasagna, 108
Beef, ground
    Stuffed Quinoa Bell Peppers, 107
Beef Stew, 135
Bell peppers
    Lemon Herb Chicken with Roasted Red Pepper
        Purée, 95
    Slow Cooker Chicken Sausage Jambalaya, 131
    Slow Cooker Vegan Chili, 132
    Steak Fajita Salad Bowl, 125
    Stuffed Quinoa Bell Peppers, 107
    Turkey Sloppy Joes, 138

Black rice
    Mango Black Sticky Rice, 159
BLT Summer Rolls, 57
Blueberries
    Baked Blueberry Quinoa Donuts, 160
    Blueberry Chia Jam, 33
    Stuffed Blueberry Pancakes, 31
Broccoli
    Shredded Broccoli Slaw, 71
Broccoli Cheese Quesadilla, 120
Brown rice
    Slow Cooker Chicken Sausage Jambalaya, 131
Brussels sprouts
    Honey Mustard Brussels Sprouts, 61
Buffalo Tofu Sticks, 110
Butternut squash
    Creamy Butternut Squash Mac & Cheese, 114
Butternut Squash Soup with Candied Pecans, 68

C
Cacao nibs
    Mint Chocolate Chip Smoothie, 145
Cacao powder
    Chocolate Peanut Butter Protein Shake, 145
Caprese Kabobs, 51
Carbohydrates, 58
Carrot Leek Soup, 66
Carrots
    Beef Stew, 135
    Slow Cooker Vegan Chili, 132
    Turkey Sloppy Joes, 138
Cauliflower
    Roasted Cauliflower and Cheddar Soup, 75
Cauliflower Tater Tots, 77
Celery
    Slow Cooker Vegan Chili, 132
Ceviche
    Salmon Avocado Ceviche, 79
    Scallop Ceviche with Grapefruit, 65
Cheese
    cheddar
        Baked Vegetarian Taco Bowls, 86
        Broccoli Cheese Quesadilla, 120
        Creamy Butternut Squash Mac & Cheese,
           114
        Roasted Cauliflower and Cheddar Soup, 75
        Turkey Sloppy Joes, 138

feta
    Chickpea Greek Salad, 123
    Watermelon Jicama Salad with Balsamic
        Reduction, 72
goat
    Fruit Pizza, 84
    Spinach Mushroom Frittata, 41
Mexican-blend
    Mexican Lasagna, 108
mozzarella
    Cheesy Turkey Meatballs, 117
    Mini Eggplant Pizza, 78
    Roasted Caprese Kabobs, 51
Parmesan
    Baked Lemon Asparagus, 83
    Creamy Butternut Squash Mac & Cheese, 114
    Kale Basil Pesto, 102
    Mini Eggplant Pizza, 78
    Sundried Tomato & Basil Frittata, 41
ricotta
    Creamy Polenta with Lemon Ricotta, 47
Cheesy Turkey Meatballs, 117
Chia seeds
    Baked Blueberry Quinoa Donuts, 160
    Blueberry Chia Jam, 33
    Kali-Fornia Smoothie, 150
    Overnight Oats, 39
    Pear Berry Green Smoothie, 149
Chicken and Waffles, 36
Chicken breast
    Balsamic Pulled Chicken, 141
    Chicken Tortilla Soup, 142
    Lemon Herb Chicken with Roasted Red Pepper
        Purée, 95
Chicken drumsticks
    Sticky Red Chicken, 105
Chicken sausage
    Slow Cooker Chicken Sausage Jambalaya, 131
Chicken thighs
    Coconut Chicken Curry, 137
Chicken Tortilla Soup, 142
Chickpea Greek Salad, 123
Chimichurri Sauce, 74
Chocolate
    Almond Joy Bites, 154
    Chunky Monkey Frozen Yogurt, 157

Cinnamon Oatmeal Stuffed Apple, 171
Granola Bars, 163
Chocolate Peanut Butter Protein Shake, 145
Chunky Monkey Frozen Yogurt, 157
Cinnamon Apple Green Smoothie, 153
Cinnamon Oatmeal Stuffed Apple, 171
Coconut
Almond Joy Bites, 154
Mango Black Sticky Rice, 159
Coconut Chicken Curry, 137
Coconut cream
Chunky Monkey Frozen Yogurt, 157
Orange Coconut Cream Smoothie, 150
Piña Colada Green Smoothie, 149
Roasted Cauliflower and Cheddar Soup, 75
Coconut milk
Mango Black Sticky Rice, 159
Mint Chocolate Chip Smoothie, 145
Coconut oil, 21–22
Cod
Fish & Kale Chips, 101
Coffee
Vanilla Coffee Shake, 146
Collard greens
Asian Collard Green Wraps, 81
Cooking tools, 27
Corn
Stuffed Quinoa Bell Peppers, 107
Cranberries
Shredded Broccoli Slaw, 71
Creamy Avocado Shake, 151
Creamy Butternut Squash Mac & Cheese, 114
Creamy Polenta with Lemon Ricotta, 47
Cucumber
Chickpea Greek Salad, 123
Green Tea Green Smoothie, 144
Steak Fajita Salad Bowl, 125

D
Dangmyeon
Korean Glass Noodles, 96
Dates
Cinnamon Apple Green Smoothie, 153
Orange Coconut Cream Smoothie, 150

E
Eggplant

Mini Eggplant Pizza, 78
Eggs
Baked Avocado & Eggs, 45
nutrition in, 44
Spinach Mushroom Frittata, 41
Sundried Tomato & Basil Frittata, 41
Sweet Potato Salad, 55
Equipment, 27

F
Fiber, 170
Fish & Kale Chips, 101
Flaxseed
Buffalo Tofu Sticks, 110
Chocolate Peanut Butter Protein Shake, 145
Granola Bars, 163
Shayna & Kiera's Strawberry Banana Smoothie, 154
Flourless Peanut Butter & Jelly Cookies, 165
Food waste, 158
French Toast, 35
Frittata
Spinach Mushroom Frittata, 41
Sundried Tomato & Basil Frittata, 41
Fruit Pizza, 84
Fully Loaded Baked Yams, 53

G
Garlic
Coconut Chicken Curry, 137
Rosemary Garlic Purple Potatoes, 58
Shrimp and Garlic Noodles, 92
Tofu Veggie Stir Fry, 99
Vegan Alfredo Sauce with Roasted Tomatoes
and Mushrooms, 111
Ginger
Coconut Chicken Curry, 137
Orange Ginger Salmon with Crispy
Quinoa Salad, 89
Gluten, 120
Glycemic Index, 58
Goji berries
Granola Bars, 163
Granola Baked Chicken and Waffles, 36
Granola Bars, 163
Grape seed oil, 22
Green Tea Green Smoothie, 144

Grilled Basil Shrimp Scampi, 106
Guacamole, 63

H
Honey Mustard Brussels Sprouts, 61
Hot sauce
    Buffalo Tofu Sticks, 110

I
Iron, 53

J
Jam, Blueberry Chia, 33
Jell-O, 169
Jicama
    Watermelon Jicama Salad with Balsamic
        Reduction, 72

K
Kabobs
    Roasted Caprese Kabobs, 51
    Teriyaki Mahi Mahi Pineapple Kabobs, 109
Kale
    Cinnamon Apple Green Smoothie, 153
    Fish & Kale Chips, 101
    Kali-Fornia Smoothie, 150
    Sausage Kale Sweet Potato Soup, 76
Kale Basil Pesto, 102
Kali-Fornia Smoothie, 150
Kitchen equipment, 27
Kiwi
    Fruit Pizza, 84
Korean Glass Noodles, 96

L
Leeks
    Carrot Leek Soup, 66
Lemongrass
    Asian Collard Green Wraps, 81
    Tofu Veggie Stir Fry, 99
Lemon Herb Chicken with Roasted Red Pepper
    Purée, 95
Lemon water, 47
Lentils
    Baked Vegetarian Taco Bowls, 86
    Slow Cooker Vegan Chili, 132

Vegan Burger, 112
Lettuce
    BLT Summer Rolls, 57
    Steak Fajita Salad Bowl, 125

M
Mac & Cheese, Creamy Butternut Squash, 114
Mahi Mahi
    Teriyaki Mahi Mahi Pineapple Kabobs, 109
Mango
    Shrimp Scampi Tacos with Mango Avocado
        Salsa, 127
Mango Avocado Sauce
    BLT Summer Rolls, 57
Mango Black Sticky Rice, 159
Maple syrup
    Almond Joy Bites, 154
    Butternut Squash Soup with Candied Pecans, 68
    Creamy Polenta with Lemon Ricotta, 47
    Korean Glass Noodles, 96
    Mango Black Sticky Rice, 159
    Orange Ginger Salmon with Crispy Quinoa
        Salad, 89
    Shrimp and Garlic Noodles, 92
Marinara with Brown Rice Pasta, 119
Mexican Lasagna, 108
Mini Eggplant Pizza, 78
Mint Chocolate Chip Smoothie, 145
Muffins, Banana Bread, 42
Mushrooms
    Korean Glass Noodles, 96
    Spinach Mushroom Frittata, 41
    Tofu Veggie Stir Fry, 99
    Vegan Burger, 112
    Vegan Alfredo Sauce with Roasted Tomatoes
        and Mushrooms, 111
Mustard
    Honey Mustard Brussels Sprouts, 61
    Shredded Broccoli Slaw, 71

N
Nonorganic foods, 25
Noodles
    Korean Glass Noodles, 96

O

Oats
  Baked Blueberry Quinoa Donuts, 160
  Cinnamon Oatmeal Stuffed Apple, 171
  Overnight Oats, 39
Olive oil, 22, 23
Olives
  Chickpea Greek Salad, 123
  Mexican Lasagna, 108
  Sweet Potato Salad, 55
Orange Coconut Cream Smoothie, 150
Orange Ginger Salmon with Crispy Quinoa Salad, 89
Organic foods, 25
Overnight Oats, 39

P

Palm oil, 22
Pancakes, 31
Panko
  Cauliflower Tater Tots, 77
  Fish & Kale Chips, 101
Pasta
  Creamy Butternut Squash Mac & Cheese, 114
  Kale Basil Pesto, 102
  Marinara with Brown Rice Pasta, 119
  Shrimp and Garlic Noodles, 92
  Vegan Alfredo Sauce with Roasted Tomatoes
    and Mushrooms, 111
Peanut butter
  Chocolate Peanut Butter Protein Shake, 145
Peanut oil, 22–23
Pear Berry Green Smoothie, 149
Pecans
  Butternut Squash Soup with Candied Pecans, 68
Pesto
  Kale Basil Pesto, 102
Piña Colada Green Smoothie, 149
Pineapple
  Piña Colada Green Smoothie, 149
  Teriyaki Mahi Mahi Pineapple Kabobs, 109
Pineapple Shrimp Wild Rice, 91
Pine nuts
  Kale Basil Pesto, 102
Pizza
  Fruit Pizza, 84
  Mini Eggplant Pizza, 78

Polenta

Polenta
  Creamy Polenta with Lemon Ricotta, 47
Portion sizes, 94
Potato
  Beef Stew, 135
  Cauliflower Tater Tots, 77
  Fully Loaded Baked Yams, 53
  Rosemary Garlic Purple Potatoes, 58
  Sausage Kale Sweet Potato Soup, 76
  Sweet Potato & Chive Cakes, 46
  Sweet Potato Salad, 55

Q

Quesadilla, 120
Quinoa
  Orange Ginger Salmon with Crispy Quinoa
    Salad, 89
  Steak Fajita Salad Bowl, 125
  Stuffed Quinoa Bell Peppers, 107

R

Rice
  Coconut Chicken Curry, 137
  Mango Black Sticky Rice, 159
  Pineapple Shrimp Wild Rice, 91
  Slow Cooker Chicken Sausage Jambalaya, 131
Roasted Caprese Kabobs, 51
Roasted Cauliflower and Cheddar Soup, 75
Rosemary Garlic Purple Potatoes, 58

S

Salad
  Orange Ginger Salmon with Crispy Quinoa
    Salad, 89
  Steak Fajita Salad Bowl, 125
  Sweet Potato Salad, 55
  Watermelon Jicama Salad with Balsamic
    Reduction, 72
Salmon
  Orange Ginger Salmon with Crispy Quinoa
    Salad, 89
Salmon Avocado Ceviche, 79
Salsa
  Baked Avocado & Eggs, 45
  Shrimp Scampi Tacos with Mango Avocado
    Salsa, 127

Stuffed Quinoa Bell Peppers, 107
Sausage
    Slow Cooker Chicken Sausage Jambalaya, 131
Sausage Kale Sweet Potato Soup, 76
Scallop Ceviche with Grapefruit, 65
Serving sizes, 94
Sesame oil, 23
Sesame seeds
    Asian Collard Green Wraps, 81
    Korean Glass Noodles, 96
    Teriyaki Mahi Mahi Pineapple Kabobs, 109
Shayna & Kiera's Strawberry Banana Smoothie, 154
Shredded Broccoli Slaw, 71
Shrimp
    Grilled Basil Shrimp Scampi, 106
    Pineapple Shrimp Wild Rice, 91
Shrimp and Garlic Noodles, 92
Shrimp Scampi Tacos with Mango Avocado Salsa, 127
Slaw, 71
Slow Cooker Chicken Sausage Jambalaya, 131
Slow Cooker Vegan Chili, 132
Smoothie
    Basil Strawberry & Watermelon Smoothie, 146
    Chocolate Peanut Butter Protein Shake, 145
    Cinnamon Apple Green Smoothie, 153
    Creamy Avocado Shake, 151
    Kali-Fornia Smoothie, 150
    Mint Chocolate Chip Smoothie, 145
    Orange Coconut Cream Smoothie, 150
    Pear Berry Green Smoothie, 149
    Piña Colada Green Smoothie, 149
    Shayna & Kiera's Strawberry Banana Smoothie, 154
    Vanilla Coffee Shake, 146
Soup
    Butternut Squash Soup with Candied Pecans, 68
    Carrot Leek Soup, 66
    Chicken Tortilla Soup, 142
    Roasted Cauliflower and Cheddar Soup, 75
    Sausage Kale Sweet Potato Soup, 76
Sour cream
    Lemon Herb Chicken with Roasted Red Pepper
        Purée, 95
Soy, 105
Soy sauce
    Korean Glass Noodles, 96
    Pineapple Shrimp Wild Rice, 91

Teriyaki Mahi Mahi Pineapple Kabobs, 109
    Tofu Veggie Stir Fry, 99
Spinach
    Mint Chocolate Chip Smoothie, 145
    Pear Berry Green Smoothie, 149
Spinach Mushroom Frittata, 41
Spring mix
    Orange Ginger Salmon with Crispy Quinoa
        Salad, 89
Squash
    Butternut Squash Soup with Candied Pecans, 68
    Creamy Butternut Squash Mac & Cheese, 114
Steak Fajita Salad Bowl, 125
Stevia, 35
Sticky Red Chicken, 105
Strawberries
    Basil Strawberry & Watermelon Smoothie, 146
    Flourless Peanut Butter & Jelly Cookies, 165
    Kali-Fornia Smoothie, 150
    Pear Berry Green Smoothie, 149
    Shayna & Kiera's Strawberry Banana Smoothie, 154
Strawberry Fruit Leathers, 167
Stuffed Blueberry Pancakes, 31
Stuffed Quinoa Bell Peppers, 107
Sundried Tomato & Basil Frittata, 41
Sunflower seeds
    Shredded Broccoli Slaw, 71
    Vegan Burger, 112
Sweet potato
    Fully Loaded Baked Yams, 53
    Sausage Kale Sweet Potato Soup, 76
Sweet Potato & Chive Cakes, 46
Sweet Potato Salad, 55
Swiss chard
    Piña Colada Green Smoothie, 149

T
Taco Bowls, 86
Tater tots
    Cauliflower Tater Tots, 77
Tea
    Green Tea Green Smoothie, 144
Teriyaki Mahi Mahi Pineapple Kabobs, 109
Toast, Avocado, 121
Tofu
    Buffalo Tofu Sticks, 110

Tofu Veggie Stir Fry, 99
Tomatoes
    Baked Vegetarian Taco Bowls, 86
    BLT Summer Rolls, 57
    Chickpea Greek Salad, 123
    Guacamole, 63
    Marinara with Brown Rice Pasta, 119
    Mexican Lasagna, 108
    Roasted Caprese Kabobs, 51
    Slow Cooker Vegan Chili, 132
    Steak Fajita Salad Bowl, 125
    storage of, 40
    Sundried Tomato & Basil Frittata, 41
    Turkey Sloppy Joes, 138
    Vegan Alfredo Sauce with Roasted Tomatoes
        and Mushrooms, 111
Tomato sauce
    Mexican Lasagna, 108
    Mini Eggplant Pizza, 78
Tools, 27
Tortilla chips
    Chicken Tortilla Soup, 142
Tortillas
    Broccoli Cheese Quesadilla, 120
    Mexican Lasagna, 108
Turkey, ground
    Asian Collard Green Wraps, 81
    Cheesy Turkey Meatballs, 117
    Mexican Lasagna, 108
    Turkey Sloppy Joes, 138
Turkey sausage
    Sausage Kale Sweet Potato Soup, 76
Turkey Sloppy Joes, 138

V

Vanilla Cinnamon Almond Butter, 33
Vanilla Coffee Shake, 146
Vegan Burger, 112
Vegan Alfredo Sauce with Roasted Tomatoes and
    Mushrooms, 111
Vitamin C, 53

W

Waffles, Chicken and, 36
Walnuts
    Chunky Monkey Frozen Yogurt, 157
Washing produce, 55
Waste, 158
Watermelon
    Basil Strawberry & Watermelon Smoothie, 146
Watermelon Jell-O, 169
Watermelon Jicama Salad with Balsamic
    Reduction, 72
Wild rice
    Coconut Chicken Curry, 137
    Pineapple Shrimp Wild Rice, 91
Wine, red
    Beef Stew, 135

Y

Yams
    Fully Loaded Baked Yams, 53
Yogurt
    Carrot Leek Soup, 66
    Chunky Monkey Frozen Yogurt, 157
    Greek
        Baked Vegetarian Taco Bowls, 86
        Chocolate Peanut Butter Protein Shake, 145
        Chunky Monkey Frozen Yogurt, 157
        Fully Loaded Baked Yams, 53
        Vanilla Coffee Shake, 146

Z

Zucchini
    Cheesy Turkey Meatballs, 117

CONVERSION CHARTS

METRIC AND IMPERIAL CONVERSIONS

(These conversions are rounded for convenience)

Ingredient	Cups/Tablespoons/Teaspoons	Ounces	Grams/Milliliters
Butter	1 cup=16 tablespoons= 2 sticks	8 ounces	230 grams
Cheese, shredded	1 cup	4 ounces	110 grams
Cornstarch	1 tablespoon	0.3 ounce	8 grams
Cream cheese	1 tablespoon	0.5 ounce	14.5 grams
Flour, all-purpose	1 cup/1 tablespoon	4.5 ounces/0.3 ounce	125 grams/8 grams
Flour, whole wheat	1 cup	4 ounces	120 grams
Fruit, dried	1 cup	4 ounces	120 grams
Fruits or veggies, chopped	1 cup	5 to 7 ounces	145 to 200 grams
Fruits or veggies, puréed	1 cup	8.5 ounces	245 grams
Honey, maple syrup, or corn syrup	1 tablespoon	0.75 ounce	20 grams
Liquids: cream, milk, water, or juice	1 cup	8 fluid ounces	240 milliliters
Oats	1 cup	5.5 ounces	150 grams
Salt	1 teaspoon	0.2 ounces	6 grams
Spices: cinnamon, cloves, ginger, or nutmeg (ground)	1 teaspoon	0.2 ounce	5 milliliters
Sugar, brown, firmly packed	1 cup	7 ounces	200 grams
Sugar, white	1 cup/1 tablespoon	7 ounces/0.5 ounce	200 grams/12.5 grams
Vanilla extract	1 teaspoon	0.2 ounce	4 grams

OVEN TEMPERATURES

Fahrenheit	Celcius	Gas Mark
225°	110°	¼
250°	120°	½
275°	140°	1
300°	150°	2
325°	160°	3
350°	180°	4
375°	190°	5
400°	200°	6
425°	220°	7
450°	230°	8